THE BEST
OF
STERLING W. SILL

Sterling W. Sill

Bookcraft
Salt Lake City, Utah

D1443497

Library of Congress Catalog Card Number: 83-71337
ISBN O-88494-486-7

First Printing, 1983

Lithographed in the United States of America
PUBLISHERS PRESS
Salt Lake City, Utah

many have been
kind enough to suggest
that my books have
lifted and encouraged
them. I hope the
selections in this
book, which are
representative of my
philosophy of life
will have that effect
on all who read
them.

Sterling W. Sill

THE BEST
OF
STERLING W. SILL

Preface

When Bookcraft suggested the publication of a compilation entitled *The Best of Sterling W. Sill* I was pleased to acquiesce. The completed project now in the reader's hands encompasses material first presented as Sunday evening radio talks over KSL in Salt Lake City and later incorporated in books. The selections include many that have received favorable comment over the years and are thus, it is hoped, favorites with the reading public.

The selections fairly represent what I may call my philosophy of life. They embody principles or qualities that to my mind are the bedrock foundations of character, whether personal or national; such qualities as honesty, integrity, faith in God, industry, truth, obedience, self-discipline, tolerance, and many others that are a part of the gospel of Jesus Christ and therefore of true Christian living. I have tried to portray these "old-fashioned virtues" in a readable style that incorporates my own personal experiences as well as stories, anecdotes, quotations, and allusions drawn from a wide range of reading.

This book is in no way endorsed by The Church of Jesus Christ of Latter-day Saints, and I accept full responsibility for its contents. Specifically I absolve the Church and its leaders from the responsibility for any error it may be found to contain.

It is gratifying to me to see these materials brought together in one volume. It is my hope that in this convenient format they will be valuable to readers of all ages and interests.

Contents

The Short Course

An interesting story is told of the experiences of a young man enrolling in college. He had some ideas about what he would like to become, and in trying to help him orient himself in his new undertaking a school counselor was going over the curriculum step by step. He was explaining to this young man the various classes that would be required for graduation and the order in which they should be taken.

The prospective student was a little impatient with the amount of work that was involved and the time that would be required in order to reach his objective. He asked his adviser, "Don't you have a short course?" The professor replied: "Oh yes, we have a lot of short courses. It all depends on just what you want to make of yourself."

Then he tried to explain to this young man some of the basic requirements in his preparation either for a professional career or for life itself. In trying to help him get a better perspective, the professor said to the young man: "When the Lord starts out to make an oak tree, he takes a hundred years to do it in, but he can make a pumpkin in ninety days." More or less, education as well as life itself is like that. And as individuals, we ourselves must choose whether we desire to become an oak tree or a pumpkin.

One of the very serious problems in our world and in our lives generally is that so frequently we are unwilling to pay the price demanded by success. The proper preparation often seems like a waste of time, so we become dropouts from education. It is often true that in our minds we want to be oak trees or even giant redwoods, but if a person is weak willed, he may end up by becoming just a pumpkin.

Because they don't understand this law of preparation, many people sacrifice their great goals, their possible capability, and their ultimate success in order to travel with the crowd along the easy path of least resistance. Benjamin Franklin once told an interesting story about a man who had a rusty ax that was so corroded by disuse that it had a dull-brown appearance. The axman wanted to have a bright, shiny ax like those of the other workmen. Accordingly, he took his ax to a grinder.

The grinder agreed to make the workman's ax sparkle like new by holding it against the grindstone, which was to be turned by the owner of the ax. The axman was very pleased, and both went to work accordingly. But putting a polish on an ax, like putting a polish on a human being, can't always be done in a minute. And after a period of long, hard turning the axman began to tire. Finally he told the grinder that he thought the ax had been ground enough. The grinder pointed out that the job was only partly done. He said to the axman, "Your ax is now only a speckled ax. Turn on, turn on, and it will be bright and shiny soon." But as weariness had set in, the axman had had a change of heart about shiny axes, and he now said, "I think I like a speckled ax best."

It is a common phenomenon to have our viewpoints change as our muscles tire or as our patience begins to wear out. A shiny ax seems much less important when it requires the "long course" of grinding. But for success in life, our minds or our spirits sometimes need to be held against the grindstone for long, hard grinding. Sometimes we become dropouts while we are still speckled with ignorance or atheism or irresponsibility, whereas if we had a little more grinding and some extra polishing, our abilities, our faith, and our self-discipline would sparkle with a satisfying radiance.

A woodsman once said that he didn't understand how his fellow workers cut down so many trees when they wasted so much time sharpening their axes. In about the same way we all tend to be more or less like the old country deacon. Someone once asked him whether or not he was a Christian. He said he was a Christian in spots. Frequently we stop turning the grindstone while we are still marred by the rust spots of our irresponsibilities, our immaturities, our insecurities, and our inferiorities. I suppose it may be better to be a spotted Christian than to be rusty all over. But life is much more profitable and pleasant if we are sharp and shiny. When we have too many rough spots interspersed with our shiny places, conflicts develop. A little longer course devoted to grinding out the rusty spots and getting rid of the corrosion can be very profitable to us.

It is helpful to remember that most of life is preparation. No one is truly happy while he is standing still or going backward. Here and hereafter we bring many problems upon ourselves when we stop turning the grindstone of preparation.

In listening to recitals of many marital problems, I have noted that most of them are caused because those involved took some variety of the short course. For example, many of the people who begin their marriages as teenagers have a pretty rough time in making a go of it, because they are not prepared. They just haven't lived long enough. It takes time to learn to build those strong foundations of basic, fundamental character. The short course does not give enough time for our personalities to mature, or to adequately build up our judgment. Frequently the short course leaves some rough spots of selfishness, laziness, irresponsibility, and lack of self-discipline.

Actually, most education is about ourselves. We study medicine to learn how to keep ourselves well physically. Psychology, psychiatry, and the other studies embracing mental and emotional health will teach us how to keep ourselves well in those respects. Agriculture is how to feed ourselves. Business is how to deal with each other. The law teaches us how to be orderly. Sociology is concerned with how we live together agreeably. And then we have that great study of religion, which shows us how to keep ourselves well spiritually.

Those people who have held their axes against the grindstone until they are no longer speckled have a great advantage in marriage or in business or in life. When we still have some rusty moral spots, or some brown spots of atheism, or some corroded spots of selfishness, or some rough spots of ignorance, or some bothersome spots of immaturity, we are found to have an increase of troubles. Life can also be pretty difficult when some spots of sloth or lethargy or indifference haven't been ground off. Someone has written:

> The man who wants a garden fair,
> Or small or very big,
> With flowers growing here and there,
> Must bend his back and dig.
>
> The things are mighty few on earth
> That wishes can attain,
> Whatever we want of any worth
> We've got to work to gain.
>
> It matters not what goal you seek,
> Its secret here reposes.
> You've got to dig from week to week
> To get results or roses.

To take the short course in planning or industry is the way we shortchange ourselves and bypass our blessings. The best course always includes the philosophy of the second mile. We need to do more than we get paid for. Someone once pointed out that "the shortest distance between two points is a straight line." Then his friend said, "Ah, but I know a shortcut." Those who tamper with premarital sex are looking for a shortcut. Those who practice dishonesty in their businesses are trying to find a shortcut. They hope to get some of life's experiences and benefits by taking a shorter route than the one provided by a straight line. All those who take shortcuts on the straight and narrow way are headed for an unhappy ending. The dope addicts are all enrolled in one of life's short courses. They don't plan on paying the price that all real success inevitably demands. They want to eat their bread before they earn it.

In fact, many don't want to earn their own bread at all. And many people want to eat the bread that others have produced. Some entire groups specialize in idleness. They don't want to work or to wait to be deserving of retirement from their jobs. They want to retire before they have worked. Many want to graduate before they have studied. By the self-delusion of dope they want to take trips into make-believe lands that do not exist. They don't want to merit the attention of their fellowmen by service and character. It is easy for some people to persuade themselves that God was wrong when in his command he said, "Six days shalt thou labour" (Exodus 20:9). And his old law of morality is now out of date, in their opinion. They have found a number of shortcuts that apparently God didn't think about when he was planning mortal life in our interest.

To some, God uttered an unintelligible concept when he said, "Be ye clean, that bear the vessels of the Lord" (Isaiah 52:11). And many people have rejected the philosophy of "peace on earth, good will toward men." They think that peace and righteousness are not as profitable as troublemaking, subversion, disloyalty, and deception. But we are on much safer ground when we understand that God did not make any mistakes when he enacted his laws, nor did he overlook anything that would be in our interests. And we had better be very careful when we try to shortcut the straight lines he has drawn, for when we bypass the law we are certain to miss the blessings.

We live in a great free land founded by God upon Christian principles. In this land, freedom, righteousness, order, and human dignity were designed to be the order of our lives. To attempt shortcuts to greater freedom in bypassing legislatures and legally constituted bodies, is to lay a snare for one's own feet. Many are taking the law into their own hands and are seeking to accomplish their ends by race riots, fear, force, clamorous demonstrations, and distorted propaganda. Although we are supposed to live in a stable, civilized, orderly society, instead of fully supporting the orderly processes of a trial by jury we have substituted such disorderly procedures as trials by marches and trials by threats or trials by race riots and troublemaking. In all of these new shortcuts in government, many Americans are changing to the short course in living, and too often they are ignoring God and leaving all thought of eternal life out of the picture.

In one of the greatest of all commands, the God of creation came down onto the top of Mount Sinai and to the accompaniment of lightning and thunder set aside one-seventh of all of the days of our lives as days to worship God, to study the scriptures, and to improve our quality of spiritual living. One of our greatest errors is that we don't want to obey this law, don't want to spend enough time in spiritual preparation, so we have drastically shortened our all-important long course in religion. As an inevitable consequence, many of us place a handicap upon ourselves comparable to the prospective doctor who severely limits his medical school experience.

An English investigator made a survey of the effort required by a bee to carry on his life's work of honey gathering. One pound of honey contains 7,000 grains of sugar, which represents the concentrated sweetness of 62,000 clover blossoms, each of which is made of up 60 florets. To obtain one pound of honey, therefore, bees must make two million, seven hundred thousand trips to and from the flowers, covering a distance of approximately five million miles. In the process of extracting the honey, the bee inserts his tiny proboscis into each separate floret, which means that he performs the operation 60 times 62,000, or three million, seven hundred and twenty thousand times, to get nectar enough to make a pound of honey.

I once heard of a hive of bees that took a short course in honey making. They gave up flowers as the source of their raw material and transferred their patronage to some discarded syrup barrels at a Coca-Cola plant. With a kind of "new morality" glee at their discovery of an abundant supply of Coca-Cola syrup, they shifted their loyalty and effort as they transferred to the short course in honey making. Their only problem was that thereafter their honey was no good and the bees themselves soon died.

A group of seagulls had a similar experience. Instead of catching their own fish, they settled down at a fish cannery, where each day they stuffed themselves with the scraps and waste discarded from the cannery. Soon they were like stuffed ducks.

They forgot how to fish and they forgot how to fly, and large numbers of them died from the occupational disease connected with their short course in fishing.

Life is the greatest commodity ever known in the universe, and making the most of it is our greatest opportunity. When the Lord said "Go to the ant, thou sluggard; consider her ways and be wise" (Proverbs 6:6), he was not recommending life's short courses. He was recommending a course that helps to prepare for eternal life.

Bunker Bean

In 1912, Harry Leon Wilson wrote a novel of some three hundred pages entitled *Bunker Bean*. This is an intriguing story of a man who was tricked into believing in himself.

Most people suffer throughout life from too mean an estimate of their own abilities. Consequently they spend their strength on small tasks and never put their real powers fairly to trial. Not to believe in God is a tragedy, but not to believe in oneself is a disaster. The human being who can have faith, who can believe in God and in himself and in his work, is fortunate indeed. One of the most powerful truths known in the world centers in the literal declaration of Jesus that "all things are possible to him that believeth" (Mark 9:23).

The study of Bunker Bean makes the potential power of belief more clearly visible, and is a part of our literature that comes under the heading of "useful fiction." All through history the myth, the fable, the allegory, have been used with great effectiveness to teach principles. A remarkable thing about the parables of the Savior is that they need not have been true as actual occurrences. Of far greater importance is that they are always true as principles and in the lessons they teach. In the parables Jesus captured many of life's vital experiences and made their messages timeless and universal in application.

Man is a child of God with abilities and potentialities so great that we seldom even suspect them, and we need more actual demonstrations of those abilities that can literally move mountains.

Bunker Bean's parents died when he was but a child, and he was left alone in the world. He "roamed the earth in rags and lived timidly through its terrors." His mind was full of fears. He was afraid of policemen; he was afraid to ride in the elevator, for each time the elevator seemed to fall he suffered the sensations of dying. He knew he was inferior to others. Some of his contemporaries made fun of him. He was afraid of the future, afraid of situations, afraid of things, afraid of life—even afraid of himself.

Then one day a false spiritualistic medium moved into the cheap boardinghouse where Bunker Bean lived. This man had a book on reincarnation, and he persuaded young Bunker Bean to believe that just as we cast off worn-out shoes and replace them with new, so we cast off our worn-out bodies and reclothe the spirit by the process of reincarnation.

Bunker Bean believed wholeheartedly in the teaching of his new-found friend. He was convinced that the friend possessed some extraordinary powers from another world. This man persuaded Bunker Bean that in return for his savings and a part of his wages over a long period, he could tell him about his (Bunker Bean's) previous incarnations.

After a considerable delay and seemingly great effort on the part of the medium, Bunker Bean was surprised and delighted to learn that he, the weak, timid Bunker Bean, had once been the great Napoleon Bonaparte, the master of Europe. It was quite a shock to learn that once people had been afraid of *him*. When he was Napoleon, Europe had trembled before him. Policemen had been as insects.

This he could not understand, so he inquired of his friend why it was that Napoleon had been so courageous and Bunker Bean so timid. The medium explained that life went in a vast karmac cycle. Napoleon had lived on the upper half of the cycle, when the qualities of courage, initiative, and power had been in the ascendancy. But Bunker Bean lived in the lower part of the cycle that was characterized by timidity, fear, and weakness. Therefore Bunker Bean possessed the exact opposite of the great Napoleonic courage and self-confidence.

But there was some wonderful news awaiting Bunker Bean. His friend told him that the lower part of the cycle was just now being completed, and he was again reentering that period in which he had lived so famously as Napoleon the Great. It would not be many days before he himself would know the truth. He would soon feel a strange life stirring within him, for he was even now well on the way to becoming his own inspired, courageous, determined self again—strong, self-reliant, fearless, and successful.

Even the *thought* of who he really was made Bunker Bean expand his chest. He straightened his shoulders and studied himself in the glass. Now that he thought about it, there was a certain majesty in his look. The thought of who he was and of his former accomplishments made him vibrate with some strange, fresh power. He went to the library, where he secured and enthusiastically read every book about Napoleon, his former self. He devoured every idea and absorbed the ambition of the mighty Bonaparte, for he, Bunker Bean, was determined to prepare himself to give full play to those great qualities which even now were beginning to reappear in his life. At all costs he must learn immediately the secrets of his previous success.

He collected pictures of Napoleon and hung them around his little attic room where he could feast his mind upon them. He imitated the speech, thoughts, and acts of his former self. He was about the same height as Napoleon, and he now remembered for the first time that he did possess some of those qualities of character that had distinguished the great general.

When he meditated and concentrated long enough he could almost remember Marengo. In those days he had been the one who had been in command. Now when he was tempted to be afraid, he thought, "What would Napoleon have done?" And he knew that Napoleon would have been contemptuous of the groundless fears which had so terrorized the early life of Bunker Bean.

One of his historians had said that Napoleon had "won battles in his tent." That was good enough for Bunker Bean. He too would plan and organize and think the problem out in advance, as Napoleon had done. He, like Napoleon, would see to it that nothing was left to chance. He would permit no exceptions to success. He had a colored picture of Napoleon sitting on his great white horse on an eminence overlooking a crucial battle which he directed with masterly waves of his sabre. Bunker Bean thrilled at the thought that this same great power still lay hidden within his own breast, just waiting for expression.

This mental stimulation proved a powerful tonic for the ailing ego of Bunker Bean. He sat up all night to read the book entitled *The Hundred Days,* which described Napoleon's battles. It told of defeat but of how gloriously his former self had taken it; of his escape from Elba, his return to France, the march on Paris, conquering by the sheer magnetism of his personality wherever he passed. His spirit bounded as he read of the frightened exit of the enemy of Napoleon, that puny usurper who went down in defeat before the mere rumor of Napoleon's approach. Then he had been magnificent! He had been willing to stake everything on his own judgment and skill. But finally there had come Waterloo and deathless ignominy. He heard again the choked sobs of "the old guard" as they bade their emperor farewell. He felt the despairing clasp of their hands as that strong bond was finally severed that had held them together those many years.

Alone in his little room high above the flaring street lights, the timid boy read *The Hundred Days* and thrilled to a fancied memory of them. Now his breath was stronger, his blood ran faster in his veins as it went to nourish a body that contained the essential portion of the great Bonaparte. Napoleon's contemporaries had called him an upstart, but the historians had said that upstarts were men who believed in themselves. This Bunker Bean now did with all his heart. As he read about himself, he forgot his mean surroundings and the timidities of spirit that had brought him thus far through life almost with the feelings of a fugitive.

Napoleon had exhibited his greatest powers as he led men to conquest. Inasmuch as there were now no wars to be fought, Bunker Bean must find some other outlet for his extraordinary ability. He had been employed in a minor position in a business undertaking. It seemed to him that this was the greatest field of adventure in which to employ his peculiar genius. Bunker Bean knew that what he had once accomplished on the field of battle he would now repeat in the field of business. He then began to think about making money. He knew nothing about the specific processes involved, but he felt sure that if he followed the principles that had been so productive in the past, he could not fail in the future.

The historians had said that Napoleon "had known human nature like a book." Therefore, he resolved to study human nature. The historian had said that "with Napoleon, to think was to act," also that Napoleon was "merciless in driving himself." Bunker Bean would now do again all of these things that had previously laid Europe at his feet.

He had been working for small pay, but as he began to think about and develop these Napoleonic qualities of initiative and courage, amazing things began to happen. He was a different person. Other people also began to take notice of the change. As a consequence, he was given more important assignments, his pay was increased, and as he began to advance with great rapidity up the positive incline of the cycle, he now knew that his friend had told him the truth.

Then he was struck by another thought. He knew that for a short period of fifty-two years he had been Napoleon. But certainly he should know about himself over a longer period. Who had he been before he was Napoleon? With these questions he again confronted his friend, and now that prosperity and money were coming his way, he could pay the medium well for whatever additional information could be obtained.

And he was not disappointed, because after the money had been paid, he learned to his further astonishment and delight that before he was Napoleon he had been the greatest of the Egyptian Pharaohs. He had had a long and wonderful reign and had died at the age of eighty-two. His death was deeply mourned by all of his people. He, Rameses, had been a ruler of great strength and character. He had been stern at times but always just. His remains received the burial customary in those times, and his body was even now interred in the royal sepulchre, covered by the sands of the centuries.

As the Pharaoh, he had been tall and handsome. He was so impressed with the account of the magnificence of the physical bearing of the Pharaoh that he immediately employed the best tailor and had his clothing cut in such a way as to give him the appearance of perfect physical development. The effect produced so improved his form that he unconsciously strove to develop the appearance that the garment gave him. He expanded his chest, drew in his waist and stood erect. "In beggar's rags most men are beggars; in kingly robes most men could be kings." He must achieve that kingly behavior that is said to distinguish royalty.

He had been thrilled by his deliberate acts of courage because they stiffened his spine. Now he would add royalty and grace and mental power. He understood that such a marked advance in his spirit could not all be made in a day. Such progress could only come after long dwelling in thought and practice upon the qualities that were responsible for his splendid past. He must do what kings did. Kings were rich. He was a king; therefore he would be rich. No sooner would his kingship be proclaimed than money would be in his hands. Money would come to him as it had come to him on the banks of the Nile many centuries before. He did not question how or when—he only knew it would come.

No longer would he play the coward before trivial adversaries. He would direct large affairs; he would think big and he would live big. Never again would he be afraid of death or life or policemen or the mockery of his fellows. His spirit grew tall and his fiber toughened. He knew he was a king, and others could not help knowing it also.

He sometimes thought about his present employer, and it occurred to him that had his employer lived with him back in Egypt he would probably have been a royal steward, a keeper of the royal granaries, perhaps, or a dependable accountant. But he could never had risen very high because his "lameness of manner was an incurable defect of the soul." He pitied his employer. Though his employer was successful and well-to-do, Bunker

Bean was in a different class. He was a king. But money and power came not only to kings, but to the kingly. Bunker Bean was born to riches; he was born a king, but he would also do the things that characterized greatness.

Strength seemed to flow to him from his mental image of the strong, calm demeanor of the Pharaoh. When reliving his previous experiences he could believe no weakness of himself. He had once ruled a mighty people in Egypt. But also centuries later he had been Napoleon and had made Europe tremble under the tread of his victorious armies. He had made some mistakes in those earlier appearances. These he would not make again. Bunker Bean believed himself to be both a wise king and a courageous soldier. *He thought courage at night and he awoke in the morning with a giant's strength. His thoughts were like a great inpouring of phosphorous into his personality. This gave him an iron will.*

Then one day Bunker Bean made a tragic discovery. The medium was a fake. None of these important things that he had believed were true. He had been cheated for the sake of his money. Then he realized that he was not a king, that he was only weak, timid Bunker Bean, mean and insignificant. What a tremendous letdown! What an occasion for discouragement, dejection, failure!

But in the years that Bunker Bean had believed himself a king, he had formed the habits that go with success, and habits are not easily broken. It was now natural and easy for him to do the things that great men did.

And then Bunker Bean had another great experience. This time he was not deceived. He learned that great scriptural philosophy that, "As [a man] thinketh in his heart, so is he" (Proverbs 23:7).

And so it had been. When he had believed himself a king, he had been a king. When he had believed himself weak, he had been weak. Had he not discovered the deception and gone on believing in himself, all would have been as before. And as he thought that through he learned this great truth: "Believing is all that matters."

Then a new truth ran through his mind, molten, luminous. No one had known that he had believed himself to be Rameses and Napoleon except himself and his former friend. But Bunker Bean had become wealthy in the years that he had lived this myth of imagining himself to be great. He had gained wealth, power, and prestige by believing in himself. Rameses and Napoleon had been only a crude bit of scaffolding on which he had climbed to success.

The confidence that he had developed in himself could now endure without the help of the scaffolding. He would still think big and live big. In spite of the discovery, his faith would still continue. The Corsican's magnetism would still prevail, and he, Bunker Bean, the lowly, would still have the power to magnetize, to thrill, to lead, and to accomplish. He would still remember that money, power, success, and leadership come not only to kings but to the kingly. The world would always be at his feet if he could only believe.

Later he visited the tomb of Napoleon to pay his tribute to the man who never lost faith in himself. Even in those last sad days on the prison rock of his lonely island, this man's spirit had remained unbroken. How greatly Bunker Bean had profited from that courage and faith! He had developed a certain grim sureness of himself which would survive.

Emotion surged into the eyes of Bunker Bean, threatening to overwhelm him. He had learned the great truth: Every man is born a king. Every man is born to riches. *To believe is all that matters.*

Acres of Diamonds

D r. Russell H. Conwell was a Union officer in the Civil War. Later he became the founder and president of Temple University in Philadelphia. In the eighty-three years of his life, which closed in 1925, he did many very praiseworthy and constructive things. But it has been said that, everything considered, the most remarkable thing in his life was his famous lecture entitled "Acres of Diamonds."

So far as is known, "Acres of Diamonds" has been the most popular single lecture ever given in the world. The five-thousandth lecture was delivered in Philadelphia, where the presentation had been made many times before, yet the proceeds from this single lecture was over nine thousand dollars and many people had to be turned away. Dr. Conwell presented the same lecture to American audiences on an average of two hundred times each year for over twenty-five years. The total income from admissions was in excess of four million dollars. Dr. Conwell used the money largely to help deserving young people acquire an education.

A substantial amount of the interest in this lecture came from Dr. Conwell himself, who was a man of great personal inspiration and accomplishment. But the lecture itself contains a great idea, and that idea is just as important now as it was in Dr. Conwell's day.

The theme of this four-million-dollar message centers around an ancient Persian farmer by the name of Ali Hafed. Ali Hafed owned a large farm made up of orchards, grain fields, and gardens. He had money out at interest, and he was a wealthy and contented man. He was contented because he was wealthy, and he was wealthy because he was contented.

But one day Ali Hafed had a visit from a Buddhist priest who was one of the best-informed men of his time. That evening the priest sat before the fire with Ali Hafed and told him about the world and how it was made. He explained that the most valuable thing in the world was a diamond. The priest explained that a diamond was a drop of congealed sunlight, a deposit of carbon from the sun. The old priest told Ali Hafed that if he had one diamond the size of his thumb, he could purchase the entire community in which he lived. And if he could find a diamond mine, he could place his children upon thrones.

After Ali Hafed had learned about diamonds, he thought of nothing else, and that night he went to bed a poor man. He had lost none of his material wealth, but he was poor now because he was discontented, and he was discontented because he now thought of himself as being poor. He now wanted diamonds more than anything else in the world. He lay awake all night thinking about these precious gems and how he could get them.

He inquired where diamonds might be found. The old priest did not know, but he told Ali Hafed that somewhere in the world there were plenty of diamonds, and all that anyone had to do was to find them. Ali Hafed made up his mind. He sold his farm, left his family in charge of a neighbor, took his money, and started out to search the world for diamonds.

He began his explorations at the Mountains of the Moon. Afterward he traveled throughout Asia. He searched in Palestine. He went on into Europe. After years of searching, his money had all been spent, and he found himself in rags, wretchedness, and poverty. One day he stood on the shores of the bay of the Strait of Gibraltar in the south of Spain as a great tidal wave came rolling in between the Pillars of Hercules. There the poor, afflicted, suffering Ali Hafed fell a victim to the awful temptation to cast himself into the incoming tide. He sank beneath its foaming crest, never to rise again.

Back home, the man who had purchased Ali Hafed's farm

was one day letting his camel drink from the garden brook. As the camel splashed its nose into the shallow water of the clear stream, its owner noted a curious flash of light coming from the white sands of the stream. He pulled out a stone that had an eye of light reflecting all the hues of the rainbow. He took the stone into his house and laid it on the mantel. Some time later when the same old priest came to visit Ali Hafed's successor, he saw the light flashing from the mantel and told the owner that this stone was a diamond. Together they rushed out into the garden and stirred up the white sands with their fingers, and lo, there came up other beautiful gems even more valuable than the first.

The above is said to be a historically true account of the discovery of the great Golconda diamond mine, the most magnificent diamond mine in history, even excelling the famous Kimberley mine itself. The Kohinoor and the Orloff diamonds of the crown jewels of England and Russia came from this mine. At the very time that Ali Hafed was longing for diamonds, he was living on top of the greatest diamond mine in the world. If he had just dug in his own garden, instead of wretchedness, starvation, and a suicidal death in a strange land, he would have literally had acres of diamonds. For every part of that old farm produced valuable gems which have since decorated the crowns of the greatest monarchs of the world.

We feel very sorry for Ali Hafed. In our minds we can see him wandering homeless and friendless further and further away from the very thing he sought so ardently. He wanted diamonds more than anything else in the world, yet he left that very thing he wanted most and exchanged it for loneliness, starvation, and death in a faraway land.

Dr. Conwell stirs up our interest and imagination with many other examples of this same principle in operation. It is probable that the main interest in Dr. Conwell's lecture was not the pathetic sight of Ali Hafed taking his leave of the very things that he wanted most. The greatest interest probably arose from the fact that the actions of Ali Hafed so much resemble the course that we ourselves so frequently take. A large percentage of our own population is continually rushing from one place to another seeking for things we never find. We stop for only a brief period and then we are on the move again. This constant unrest is caused by a strange inclination among us to think of success and happiness as lying in some distant country, to be found only under unusual circumstances. The grass usually looks so much greener on the other side of the fence that it draws our attention and our interest away from those more important things that lie right under our noses. We look for some great deeds to do in some faraway foreign land and we neglect our own acre of diamonds with all the possibilities that are just begging to be uncovered in our own back yard.

This four-million-dollar lecture suggests that most of our opportunities are not found in the distance, but usually in the vicinity of our birth. In fact, opportunity may be found wherever one really digs for it and usually in no other place. Henry Ford found acres of diamonds by digging in his own tool shed. Thomas A. Edison found his acres of diamonds in the experiments of his own laboratory. The people of two thousand years ago believed that no good could come out of Nazareth, yet Jesus went from the carpenter shop to become the Savior of the world. Despite these and many other outstanding examples, however, how futile it sometimes is to urge a person to start digging in his own home town and make good right where he is! The chances always seem so much better if we could cultivate the distant acres that lie beyond our reach.

We sometimes feel that we would be great if only we could be elected to some important political office or by some other means have the power of exceptional accomplishment placed in our hands by someone else. The truth is that if we would dig a little deeper in our own back yard we would find some important, inspiring purpose for our own lives. It is a serious mistake to wait for some great deeds to do in the future when there are so many little deeds that need to be done in the present.

In the early days of this country many people lost their lives in the gold rush across the Great American Desert on their way to California. The same thing happened in the Arctic wastes of the Yukon, while those who died frequently had left great undeveloped treasures in their own home towns. Some of us never become aware of our greatest treasures. The most likely place to look for diamonds is under our own feet and within ourselves. In fact, God has implanted in every man the very things that he seeks. If you seek the kind of faith that moves mountains, look within yourself, for God has already implanted in your own heart the seeds of faith and power, and these are waiting only for you to make them grow. If you seek the courage that will make you one of the giants of your day, don't look in Barcelona or Paris or London, for it is already within yourself awaiting only your command. Every man has within himself a vein of greatness. He has only to learn to command the shaft that draws out the gold.

One young man said he would like to be an orator but that no one would elect him to an office great enough for his talents to be utilized. If you want to be an orator, start speaking your piece now. Oratory is not bestowed by political election or special appointment. Oratory as well as office depends on how well you have developed those particular acres inside yourself. Those who are not great before they get into office will not be great when they get in. Just begin digging where you are and you will be surprised what will turn up. Demosthenes had a speech defect, but he started to dig and he finally became the greatest orator in the world, not in spite of his speech defect but because of it. His defect made him learn to dig.

Dr. Conwell tells of meeting Fred Douglass, the Black orator and journalist of American slave days, who six months before his birth was pledged by his white master to a creditor in payment of a debt. And for the first part of his life Fred Douglass did not even own his own body. Then some friends of his took up a collection of $750 and purchased Fred Douglass and made him a present of himself. The father of Fred Douglass was a white man, his mother was a Negro slave. Mr. Douglass said, "I never saw my father, and I remember very little of my mother, except that once she tried to keep an overseer from whipping me, and the lash cut across her face and spilt her blood over me." The plot in life that Fred Douglass was asked to cultivate did not at first seem very promising, but he dug long and deep and uncovered his own acres of diamonds.

But the story of Fred Douglass is in one way the story of every man. We first need to get possession of ourselves. In the beginning God gave man dominion over everything upon the earth, including himself, and when we really start taking possession things begin happening. Shakespeare had Cassius say: "The fault, dear Brutus, is not in our stars/But in ourselves, that we are underlings." Life did not really intend that Demosthenes should be a poor speaker, just because it gave him a speech impediment. The defect was just to stimulate him to dig. It is all wrong to allow a weakness to become permanent.

Dr. Conwell tells of a man who used to sit on his front porch and smoke away his wife's small income in idleness. Then this man would get up in prayer meeting and ask sympathy for what he called the Lord's poor. Dr. Conwell said that he thought the Lord was not very pleased with this kind of poor people. We must not mistake sloth, ignorance, and indifference for humility and piety. God wants all of us to be numbered among the Lord's rich, otherwise he would not have hidden so many wonderful gifts within us.

Dr. Conwell said that the very apex of his life's thought was that people should do their best right where they are with the wonderful gifts that God has already given them. He said: "Arise, ye millions of Americans. Trust in God and believe in your opportunities and in yourselves." Dr. Conwell's principle of greatness will work for everyone. Whatever you have to do, put your whole mind and soul into its doing. The greatest of all wealth is eternal life, and this too comes by this vigorous digging process. As Jesus said, "see that ye serve him with all your heart, might, mind and strength, that ye may stand blameless before God at the last day" (D&C 4:2).

Ali Hafed sought for diamonds because he believed them to be the most valuable things in the world, but Jesus urged a higher standard upon us. He told his apostles: "Seek ye first the kingdom of God and his righteousness; and all these things [life's necessities] shall be added unto you" (Matthew 6:33).

Jesus also said the kingdom of God is within us; and that is where most of the digging needs to take place. A little of the light and glory of God in our lives dwarfs into insignificance all of the brilliance that came from Ali Hafed's brook. It is a great day in our lives when we determine to dig a little deeper into the acre that God has given into our personal care.

Under the Circumstances

Dr. Leon Tucker, a great teacher of the Bible, used to tell a story of a lady with poor health. As her friends would ask her how she was, she would usually say, "I am feeling as well as could be expected, under the circumstances." In making a comparison to another kind of poor health, Dr. Tucker said that far too many Christians also allow themselves to live "under the circumstances," whereas at our best we should live "above" and "ahead of" the circumstances.

When someone asked Napoleon, "How are conditions?" he replied, "I make conditions." And only as we ourselves rise above our environment can we reach our greatest potential. During a severe storm, the conqueror of Europe said to his ship's captain, "Fear not, thy boat carries Caesar."

When we fail to live above our circumstances, we bring upon ourselves a great many problems. A middle-aged man came a long distance to talk with me about some of his difficulties. He felt impelled to make a long confession of his many sins and weaknesses. But when asked what he was going to do when the next temptation presented itself, he said: "I don't know. I can't tell what I will do until I know what the circumstances are going to be."

Here is a man who is continually lamenting his weaknesses to others but who has never learned to do anything about correcting them. Someone has said that we should never consider how much the devil tempts, but rather how strongly we are inclined. Against his better judgment, this man has allowed a very serious inclination toward evil to grow up within himself. He is ashamed of his sins and realizes that his eternal life depends upon himself, yet before making up his mind about what he will do he must wait to discover what the pressures are going to be. Like many of us, he gives the control of his life over to whatever conditions he may happen to meet along life's way.

One of the most serious problems of our lives is our willingness to be governed by conditions. We are inclined to imitate the attitudes of the weathercock, which waits to see which breeze is going to blow before it decides on its own directions. We also see our own likeness at its worst pictured in the chameleon that can't tell what his color is going to be until he learns which environment he will be in.

In the beginning God gave man dominion over everything upon the earth, including his circumstances and himself. Therefore it must be disturbing to God when we turn over that dominion to our surroundings. God's animal creation is always true to its own instincts. We have never heard of a crime wave turning a group of horses from their natural destiny. Nor have we discovered any upswings in the divorce rate of a flock of sparrows. But animals are allowed no deviation from the natural laws governing their lives. Only to man did God say, "Thou mayest choose for thyself" (Moses 3:17).

Our free agency is probably our greatest gift from God, and we should not abandon this birthright in order to conform to the less worthy examples around us. There is an interesting story about circumstance told about the early explorers who came to the western continent after Columbus. They found a group of aborigines practicing the peculiar custom of making little rolls of the dried leaves of a certain slow-burning plant. One end of this roll they put into their mouths. Then they lit a fire on the other end, and spent their time inhaling the fumes.

After watching the Indians with lighted torches in their mouths, the explorers took over the idea, and it has since become one of America's largest industries. We presently employ some of the world's best advertising brains to induce men, women, and children to adopt the custom. By the way of implementation we appropriate thousands of acres of our most fertile soil, a substantial part of our financial resources, and a large share of the human energy of the world's greatest nation to circulate tobacco smoke through our lungs and blow it out through our noses. And even though we have now discovered that the custom of these primitive Red Men costs us a lot of misery and thousands of deaths every year, the practice goes on undiminished.

When we associate with someone who smokes we frequently feel that under the circumstances we should smoke also. Or when someone also breathes the air of dishonesty we are often influenced to take up *that* habit.

One of the most powerful phrases in the world is, "Everybody's doing it." When others are immoral, then "under the circumstances" that seems like the thing to do. Or when everyone else is profane, why shouldn't we be? We continue to corrupt ourselves in a thousand different ways because others are doing it. It is because we live so much under the circumstances that our great American community of Christians has become a nation of lawbreakers, alcoholics, and transgressors of the laws of God.

There is an interesting phrase repeated frequently in the Book of Mormon that says (with merely alteration of the year number) "And in the . . . sixty and seventh year the people began to grow . . . wicked" (Helaman 6:16). It seems that they all more or less got the idea at about the same time. During the next few years their wickedness continued to increase at about the same rate until some conflicting circumstance brought them back to their senses. Then for a time a more or less uniform trend went in the other direction. These group movements are still taking place. More or less we all seem to go up and down the ladder together. There is an upsurge in human delinquency going on in the eastern part of the United States. But the same upsurge is also taking place in the western part of the United States. And it is also going on in every other part of the United States. Whether the example we see is good or bad, wise or foolish, we tend to be influenced by it.

It is very interesting to watch the graph made by the ups and downs of the stock market. On Monday and Tuesday the stock market indexes went up, then for no good reason on Thursday and Friday they went down. If the president has a heart attack, as a consequence the price of our listed securities drops many billions of dollars, wiping out a substantial percentage of their total value. When President Kennedy was shot, the market took a serious tumble. This price movement had nothing to do with any actual changes in the values of the securities themselves. To that extent to which the stock market, like the human beings behind it, lives "under the circumstances," then to that extent the actions of both become largely unpredictable.

A salesman once said to his boss, "I think I did pretty well under the circumstances." His boss said, "What in the world are you doing down there?" That is a good question, and it reminds us of the individual who said, "For a jerk I think I have come quite a long way."

A landlady was once trying to rent her spare room to a stranger. After apologizing for some of the disadvantages of the room she said, "But as a whole, don't you agree it's a pretty good room?" The prospective occupant said, "Yes, as a hole I think it's perfect, but as a place to live in I'm not very favorably impressed." It might be said that as "a hole" *we* are doing pretty well, but as children of God, formed in his image, and heirs to his glory, we still have a long way to go.

Probably the best place to start this important journey to success would be to get out from under the circumstances. There is no particular logic in getting drunk and making fools of ourselves merely because someone else is doing it. If a thing is wrong, to say "Everybody's doing it" doesn't make it right any more now than when the people said it in the days of Sodom and Gomorrah. It doesn't make any more sense to lose our souls now, because everybody's doing it, than it did in the days of Noah.

The eternal laws of God were given us to live under by him who created us. To obey these laws is the best way to live regardless of the circumstances—above them, in fact. Someone has said that it doesn't matter very much what is behind us, or what is before us, the thing that is important is what is inside of us and what we do about it.

The psychologists tell us that one of the greatest weaknesses among young people today is their unwillingness to personally accept the responsibility for their own failures and shortcomings. But that is also one of the greatest weaknesses in adults. We often try to justify ourselves by what is around us. What we need to understand is that above the dictators and above chance and above circumstance there is God, the author of righteousness who is also the author of reason, happiness, and justice. He has endowed his children with his own potentialities and has placed them under his law. If we live it as we should, we may bring about the greatest objective of life, which is our own eternal exaltation. But if we refuse the law of God and make ourselves subject to circumstances, then we have only to depend upon chance to save our souls. It has been pointed out that unless we get within us the will of the God who is above us, we will soon be yielding ourselves to that which is about us. We ourselves must accept the responsibility for ourselves, for God is still unalterably committed to the idea that we must abide the result of our own choices.

Someone has expressed a very helpful philosophy as follows:

The Will

You *will* be, what you will to be;
Let failure find its false content
In that poor word *environment*,
But spirit scorns it, and is free.

Will masters time, it conquers space,
It cows that boastful trickster chance
And bids the tyrant circumstance
Uncrown, and fill a servant's place.

The human will, that force unseen,
The offspring of the deathless soul,

Can hew the way to any goal,
Though walls of granite intervene.

Be not impatient in delay,
But wait as one who understands;
When spirit rises and commands
The gods are ready to obey.

Our forefathers came to this country that they might find and worship God. They have helped to provide this great heritage that we call freedom. But what kind of freedom is it? Are we looking only for the freedom to follow the crowd? Is the objective we seek the freedom to be immoral or the freedom to be atheists or the freedom to follow the path of least resistance and participate in a giant crime wave? What good does it do to call God our Father, if we then go our own way as though we were orphans? This country was not founded as a place where we could merely do as we pleased and follow the path of least resistance. It was founded as a place where we could be free to worship God, a place where we could take our part in his program of righteousness and bring about the celestial glory of our own souls.

One night as a little girl was getting into her bed she said to her mother, "Tell me the story of Jesus with me in it." The greatest of all accomplishments is the story of Jesus when we are in it. The picture can never be complete if we leave ourselves out. The earth itself was created as a place for us to work out our eternal exaltation in fear and trembling before God. The most important idea in the universe is for us to stick to our inheritance and put ourselves into God's great program to the very limit. We should make it completely relevant to every detail of our lives. It must have significant meaning for us right now. Already we have allowed our lives to lose too much of their importance because we have chosen to live under the circumstances.

Julius Caesar was once captured by a tribe of barbarians. They told him that they were holding him for a fifty-thousand-dollar ransom. Caesar laughed at his captors because they did not know the value of their prisoner. Caesar advised them to raise the ransom figure by at least ten times. A part of our problem is that we are holding the value of our lives and the importance of our experience at too low a figure even in our own minds. We were designed for better things than to go around blowing tobacco smoke on people or becoming irresponsible alcoholics or being that kind of weak-kneed Christian who can only live "under the circumstances."

Our greatest destiny and happiness will never be achieved as lawbreakers or sinners or the victims of events. The wise man Solomon pointed out our greatest opportunity when he said, "Let us hear the conclusion of the whole matter: Fear God, and keep his commandments: for this is the whole duty of man" (Ecclesiastes 12:13). This should also be our greatest pleasure.

Growth Rings

In our backyard we have a large cross section of a petrified tree. It is like flint in hardness. The grains of the wood are still natural in appearance, with beautiful colors shining out from the tree's face. Apparently this particular section of tree has lain exposed to the elements for many generations, and the rains of the centuries have given it a brilliant luster so that it resembles the artificially polished, many-colored, jewelry-like pieces of petrified wood that are sometimes sold in novelty stores. Besides being filled with beautiful polished colors, the tree's yearly growth rings are all visible in its surface.

My interest in this tree was increased when I read a study made of the stump of a giant redwood. A count of its growth rings indicated that the tree was nearly three thousand years old. And to make the tree's history a little more graphic, those making the report had marked in a picture of the stump that particular growth ring that was being formed while some important historical event was taking place. Then some external drawings had been made showing the tree's size at various times throughout its history. One picture showed the tree as it was when the Revolutionary War was being fought. A slightly smaller tree indicated its size when Columbus discovered America. It was a little smaller yet at the time of the fall of the Roman empire. Even when Jesus was being born in Bethlehem this tree was an impressive giant, over a thousand years old. With some of these thoughts in mind, I sometimes look into the face of the tree in our backyard and wonder when it lived and how many great historical sights it witnessed.

The growth rings themselves tell an interesting story of alternating periods of favorable and unfavorable living conditions. There were some years when the new wood added during that year was a quarter of an inch in thickness. Then a series of drouth years or other unfavorable conditions followed when the tree grew only a small fraction of that amount. I think of the Bible's account of Egypt's seven fat years followed by seven lean years in the days of Joseph.

Sometimes, as I try to read the history of my tree, I also think about the ups and downs in my own life, and the favorable and unfavorable experiences in the lives of other people. I thought what an interesting experience it would be if we could see the year-by-year growth records as we are actually making them in our own lives. If we understood the amount and the consequences of our personal growth, we might be motivated more effectively to make each year's growing conditions as favorable as possible so we could produce a reasonable amount of new wood each year.

No good businessman would neglect to keep an accurate year-by-year record of his financial progress. At the end of each year, he adds up the gains and subtracts the losses in order to discover what his net growth has been for that year. Most businessmen also have a graph showing the year-by-year progress made in their net worth. Doctors keep records of their patients for shorter periods on hourly temperature charts and blood-pressure reading sheets. The doctor also likes to know whether the patient is gaining or losing weight and how much.

God is also keeping some gain-and-loss charts for us. We remember that Belshazzar, the unrighteous king of Babylon, was found to be a spiritual lightweight on the Lord's scales. But Belshazzar himself knew nothing about it until the mysterious hand wrote his final score in the plaster of the palace wall. It said: "God hath numbered thy kingdom, and finished it. Thou art weighed in the balances, and art found wanting. Thy kingdom is divided and given to the Medes and the Persians." (Daniel 5:26-28.) If Belshazzar had had some accurate way of recording his gains and losses as he went along, he might not have been so badly taken off guard.

Even those who handle important stock market operations would be lost without an accurate record of ups and downs. Men dealing with money or elections think it is very important to be able to see the actual gains and losses, booms and depressions, inflations and deflations, as they are actually taking place. When we can see trends and understand their significance, we are in a much better position to do something about them. Joseph was only able to save his people from starvation because he knew in advance that the seven good years would be followed by seven years of drouth, and because he was willing to do something about it. And Belshazzar could have prevented his own destruction if he had kept an accurate record showing in which direction he was going.

This information is just as necessary for us, and it would be interesting as well as helpful to see some graphic representations of our own spiritual peaks and valleys. If we were sufficiently advised about our own moral depressions, and the upswings and downdrafts in our conduct before God, then we could identify on our charts the influences that caused our highs and lows. We could then understand where and why they started, and when and how they were stopped. Then we could point to our graph and say, "Here is where I was at my best"; or we might say, "This long valley of depression marks that difficult battle I had with myself." Then we would know the effect of a negative attitude or the cost of some bad habit. We could see where we stumbled over a particular obstacle or fell flat before some specific temptation. Certainly with such a graphic statement of profit and loss always before us, we could greatly improve the spiritual solvency of our lives.

If we are to reach a maximum of success, we must know what makes our effectiveness go up and down and, of course, we should also know what our scores are at all times and what should be done about them. The extremes of our fluctuations are

illustrated by a UPI dispatch reporting a kind of Horatio Alger
success story in reverse. The newspaper headline said, "A Hero
on Sunday, a Bum on Monday." It recalled that on the previous
Sunday, twenty-eight-year-old John Dennis had rescued eleven-
year-old Ronnie Perez from the tracks of the Long Island railroad
freight yard. His clothing had caught fire, and while fifty
passersby watched the burning boy, only Dennis had been willing to do anything about it. From his hospital bed Ronnie had
asked his mother to thank Mr. Dennis, and he added, "May God
bless him."

But fifteen hours later Dennis was picked up by the police
for robbing a Brooklyn service station. The arresting officer said:
"Dennis was a hero in the morning and a bum at night." Judge
Herbert I. Sorin said to Dennis, "I was very proud of you yester-
day morning, but I am ashamed of you now." This is something
like what God said to Belshazzar.

Our own indicators of success and failure may go up and
down a little less dramatically, but just the same, if we were
intelligently aware of our spiritual fluctuations and the changes in
our moral temperatures, our lives could be kept under better control.

The scriptures say that everyone will be judged according to
his works. And the Supreme Judge of the world is not only all-
wise and all-knowing but also a good accountant, and he has an
unerring record of our upsurges and our backslidings. We could
make a much better final score if we kept track of it as we went
along. It is very strange that so many people who get involved in
some serious problems claim that they don't even know what is
causing their difficulty and therefore they can do nothing about
it. Some people actually become moral bankrupts and say they
are not aware of the reasons for their insolvency.

One of our most unfavorable statements of position is
described by the confused individual who says, "I'm all mixed
up." It seems so easy to get our goals mixed up, our directions
mixed up, and right and wrong mixed up. We get our sins mixed
up with our ambitions, our faith mixed up with our inferiority
complexes. We get too many civil wars going on inside of us, and

sometimes we haven't the slightest idea of who is winning. How can it be otherwise if we fail to keep score and have no altimeter to register our ups and downs and no compass to tell us which way we are going? Someone has pointed out that there are actually five primary directions: there are north, south, east, and west, and the fifth direction is where we are now. Even the best compass may not help us very much until we get ourselves located, and the most accurate speedometer will be of little use unless we are headed in the right direction. We should first find ourselves, then get ourselves unmixed and headed toward the right goal at the right speed.

Self-preservation is said to be the first law of nature, and everyone's life is now at stake. We not only have a natural hunger to survive physically, but we have an even more important hunger to live eternally. For this purpose, God has given this self-preservation urge a natural companion, which has been referred to as our growth instinct. Everyone has an inborn yearning for improvement. At its best it is a natural hunger to be like God.

The Creator himself has implanted in every soul "an upward reach," urging him upward and onward forever. Every soul is homesick and restless for eternal life. The conscience of man is always encouraging him to be better than he is, and the still small voice of the Spirit is like a radar beam guiding him heavenward. But in spite of all these uplifting influences, it is probably true that the most neglected resource in the universe is our own human resource. We have our automobiles regularly washed, shined, inspected, and repaired. We take the most scientific care of our crops and herds. But frequently we are far less thoughtful about ourselves. That is, we often fail to give ourselves the kind of education that we should have, and frequently we so badly neglect our spiritual welfare that a yearly spiritual growth ring is almost indiscernible. Sometimes we actually throw our growth instinct into reverse gear by filling our lungs with nicotine and saturating our tissues with booze. Our growth rings also lose ground when our minds are steeped in dishonesty, our mouths filled with profanity, our hearts loaded with hate, and our eyes hungry with lust. Sin causes our crime waves to mount and our delinquency graph to shoot upward and our growth rings to disappear. Our guilt complexes cause us to lose confidence in ourselves; sin weakens our faith and enfeebles our courage. When we sell ourselves short by withdrawing our industry and abandoning ourselves, our eternal score begins a fatal drop.

Recently I had an unpleasant experience of sensing a negative, miserable attitude in a former acquaintance who was now at the extreme end of his seven poor years. He had just been released from a Church assignment which he had held for ten years. When he was asked to say a few words to the assembled congregation, he began by saying, "I am just as frightened to stand before you today as I was when I stood up here to accept this position ten years ago." Then for the next fifteen minutes he breathed out over two thousand people the most negative, belittling, pitiful, self-depreciating kind of ideas. In substance he said, "I am just as frightened and just as ignorant and just as weak and just as sinful and just as no-account as I was ten years ago," and it was clearly evident that he was not exaggerating. We have no business being as frightened or as sinful or as worthless as we were ten years ago. God will hold us responsible for the abuse of this growth instinct that he has entrusted us with. Certainly he did not give it to us to mock him.

So far as our talents are concerned, disuse is as mortal a sin as abuse, and just as destructive. The most bitter denunciation that Jesus ever poured out upon the head of anyone was upon the unprofitable servant who hid his talent in the ground. Jesus was kind to the repentant adultress; he had a sympathetic interest with the thief on the cross who wanted to do better; but to the poor unfortunate who said, "I was afraid, and went and hid my talent in the earth." Jesus said, "Thou wicked and slothful servant." Then he said, "Take . . . the talent from him and give it unto him which hath ten talents. . . . And cast ye the unprofitable servant into outer darkness: there shall be weeping and gnashing of teeth." (Matthew 25:25, 26, 28, 30.) Jesus meant for us to put talents to work; he meant for us to get the maximum benefit from our growth instincts.

Some time ago a chief justice of a state supreme court made an interesting speech entitled, "What I Would Do If I Were Twenty-one Again." Among other things he said, "I would take as good care of myself as I do my automobile," and as part of himself he included his health, his appearance, his spirit, his mental attitude, and his eternal soul.

One of the tragedies of life is that frequently we seem to have a greater appreciation of the values in our automobiles than we do of those in our eternal lives. Yet what an exciting thought it ought to be to understand that the greatest values in the universe are those eternal gifts inside of us, and that we ourselves may determine what their increases will be for eternity! Every human being is also a human becoming, and this important science of improving ourselves and becoming like God will always be the most important work of the world. In fact, this is the work in which God himself spends his entire time, as he has said: "This is my work and my glory, to bring to pass the immortality and eternal life of man" (Moses 1:39).

As we make the religion of Christ an important part of our lives, it also becomes *our* work and *our* glory to bring to pass the immortality and eternal life of man. In this effort may God help us to perfect our timetable for putting some good yearly growth rings on our lives.

Letters of Credit

Someone once said that the greatest invention of all time took place when the Phoenicians invented money. As soon as we had an acceptable medium of exchange, our ability to trade freely and profitably with each other began to skyrocket.

However, an even greater advance occurred when someone figured out the process of credit. Credit enables a young married couple to establish a family even without much money. They can own a home now in the time of their greatest need, rather than twenty or thirty years in the future. Students can better prepare for their life's work because of credit.

Cities, states, nations, business organizations, and churches frequently carry on many of their most important activities on credit. This interesting word is derived from a term meaning to "trust" or to "believe in." And it describes many of our most important activities. The schools give us credit when we satisfactorily complete a course of study. The bank gives us credit when we make a deposit in a savings account. Our friends give us credit when we do those things that are right and proper. Even God operates on a system of credits and debits. The scripture says that in the final judgment the books will be opened and everyone will be judged according to his works.

But life also keeps a very interesting set of books in the person of each individual himself. When one develops a good character trait, life gives him credit. If he obeys the laws of health, the fact is registered in the individual. If he develops wisdom, industry, and fairness in his dealings, these are recorded in the personality in such a way that everyone may know the amount of his balance. In many cases we actually speak of the individual himself as a credit. We say that he is a credit to his family, a credit to his business, a credit to his church, a credit to his country, and even a credit to God.

When the banker speaks of a credit balance, he means the amount by which our credits exceed our debits. Based on this right to be trusted, a financial institution sometimes issues "letters of credit" in a person's name. These letters are signed by some responsible officer of the bank, who certifies that the person named is entitled to draw on the bank up to a specified limit.

But life makes out the more valuable letters of credit. These are also based on our right to be trusted and believed in. But life's letters of credit are unique inasmuch as they are not written on paper but in us. They can be read in our faces, our manners, our words, and even our bodily movements. And just as a good bookkeeper can tell how much credit one has in the bank, so one skilled in the language of human lives can read the letters of credit manifest in the voice, the eyes, the expression, and the spirit.

The story is told that on one occasion President Abraham Lincoln was considering a certain man as a possible member of his cabinet. The individual under consideration was being urged by one of Lincoln's advisors. When Lincoln turned the man down his advisor asked him why. The President said, "I don't like his face." His advisor said, "You can't hold the poor man responsible for his face." But President Lincoln replied, "Every man is responsible for his face." It gives us something to think about that every experience and every attitude and every ability has a way of registering itself in the individual himself. What every man is soon gets into his face, his brain, and his nervous system.

While Jesus was being tried in the palace of Caiaphas the high priest, Peter tried to keep his own identity a secret, but he could not even fool the servant girl. And when he tried to deny his connection with Jesus, he got himself in still deeper, and one of his accusers said, "Surely thou also art one of them; for thy speech [betrayeth] thee" (Matthew 26:73).

For that matter, everything about us betrays us. Even the lie detector knows whether or not we are telling the truth. It is thought that ideas make engrams in the gray matter of the brain; they also cause changes to take place in the spirit and in the body. For example, when a person becomes insanely angry you can actually see the rage in his face. If you take a photograph at that instant the camera will also see it, and it will record the passion on paper. Our thoughts and emotions actually mold our features. After the passion has passed, the features are released from its grip, but they may never fully return to their original form. As the passion is repeated, the features take on more and more the permanent appearances of the passion by which they have been moved.

The science of crime detection suggests that no one can pass through a room without leaving some evidence of his having been there. Similarly no attitude, thought, or sin can pass through our lives without leaving its visible tracks. We can actually *see* lust, greed, selfishness, and dishonesty; and the visage of each such evil is repulsive.

Of course, our lives deal in both negative and positive bookkeeping. When a person is extremely happy his eyes sparkle, there is an indescribable glow in his countenance, his spirit throws off a kind of beneficent radioactivity in letters of light that everyone can read. Righteousness is always beautiful, and it builds us in its image.

Brigham Young once said: "I shall see the time when I can converse with this people without speaking. The expression on my countenance will tell the congregation what I wish to convey." But even now God can read our lives, as every virtue and every ability and every thought is a part of his bookkeeping in us.

Frances Parkinson Keyes, author of *Face and Fortune,* tells about her publisher's request that she have some new photographs taken. Mrs. Keyes did not like to be photographed, but she knew that her publisher could not use the old photograph forever, and she consented to have a new one taken. When it was finished Mrs. Keyes compared it with the one taken twenty-five years earlier. Her new picture gave her feminine vanity an acute shock. She did not like the idea of being presented to her public as she presently was. Her first thought was to have the prints touched up a bit. But she knew that people who painted their faces or touched up their pictures didn't fool anyone but themselves. A far better way to change one's face is to touch it up from the inside. Mrs. Keyes said, "A quarter of a century of effective living should put something better into a woman's face than wrinkles and an unwelcome roll under her chin." In a quarter of a century one usually gets intimately acquainted with pleasure and pain, joy and sorrow.

We struggle and succeed or we get discouraged and fail. We lose or gain in courage and faith. We should be wiser, more gentle, more patient, and more tolerant, as a result of living. Our sense of humor should mellow our outlook, and our sympathies should get deeper, but we may be sure in any event that everything, good or bad, will be faithfully recorded in the individual. And when a person tries to artificially erase the debit marks of age, he may also destroy the credit signs of character and experience.

Mrs. Keyes quotes Shakespeare's famous line from *Hamlet:* "This above all,—to thine own self be true;/And it must follow as the night the day,/Thou canst not then be false to any man." As we are true to ourselves or to anyone else, more funds are placed at our disposal in the bank of life. Emerson says, "It is one of the most beautiful compensations of life that no one can sincerely try to help another without helping himself." Kind deeds place a substantial credit to our account. Right thinking is a credit. A good character is a credit. Living the great Christian principles always increases our credit balance. The very presence of a man sometimes gives us confidence in him. His face is a promise to pay. Some people never disappoint. Their character and ability are honored wherever they go with a kind of credit that is preferred by the bank above any third-party endorsement.

As to character, ability, and industry, someone has written:

There's a man in the world who is never turned down
Wherever he chances to stray;
He gets a glad hand in the populous town,
Or out where the farmers make hay.
He's greeted with pleasure on deserts of sand
And deep in the aisles of the woods.
Wherever he goes there's a welcoming hand
For the man who delivers the goods.

An employer once advertised for a boy to assist him in his office, and nearly fifty boys applied. Quickly the employer chose one and sent the rest away. An associate asked, "Why did you choose that boy when he didn't have a single recommendation?" The employer said: "You are mistaken; he had a great many recommendations. He wiped his feet and closed the door after him when he came in, showing that he was orderly and tidy. He instantly gave up his seat to the lame man, showing that he was kind. He took off his cap and answered my questions promptly and respectfully, showing that he was polite.

"He lifted up the book which I had purposely laid on the floor, and placed it on the table, while all the others stepped over it, or shoved it aside. This shows that he was thoughtful. He waited quietly for his turn, instead of pushing the others aside, showing that he was modest.

"When I talked with him, I noticed that his hair was combed, his clothes were brushed, and his teeth were white as milk. When he wrote his name, I observed that his fingernails were clean, instead of being tipped with jet, like those of the handsome little fellow in the blue jacket."

Such characteristics are the finest letters of recommendation, and they can tell more in ten minutes about a boy's worth than all the letters that could be assembled.

But sometimes our actions write letters of *discredit.* When we develop unfavorable attitudes or bad character traits they are all shown in our life's balances. An unfavorable reputation makes one appear like a sailor wearing an unsightly tattoo that he can't hide, and his weaknesses will go on producing discredit and distrust in the minds of others.

Hippocrates once said that the most dangerous maladies are those that disfigure the countenance. Every evil is ugly and every sin tends to tranform us into its likeness. Every thought of sensuality or dishonesty that we entertain becomes a part of us and tends to weaken and destroy us.

If you overstrain a piece of steel or overstretch a piece of elastic, it never quite recovers. In much the same way, foreign matter in the mind and heart produces distortions which we never quite get over. These are influences we can't hide. If one is feebleminded, the fact registers itself in the features. It is a mental tattoo that cannot be hidden. Each time the soul is distorted by evil, the disfiguration becomes greater and more permanent.

Certainly God needs no recording angel to look over our shoulder and write down our misdeeds. They are all engraved in the depths of our souls and advertised through the show windows of our faces. The scriptures indicate that every one of us will eventually find his own place in one of the degrees of glory in a place that exactly fits his life. It won't help us very much then to paint our faces or try to hide the tattoo that sin has etched into our souls. It will be perfectly evident to everyone then, which souls are celestial and which are telestial. No plastic surgery is a very good creator of real health and beauty.

Someone has said that beauty is only skin deep, but that refers merely to external appearance. The most thrilling beauty is not on the outside. The most wonderful plastic surgery takes place when we get the right kind of ideas and impulses into the machinery of our lives. God runs the most effective beauty parlor ever known in the world.

Socrates prayed, "Make me beautiful within." We can make ourselves beautiful by holding in our minds and hearts beautifying thoughts. We have all seen plain people who have become beautiful by the working of radiant spirituality. A godly spirit will make the plainest body beautiful. Great mental and spiritual qualities transform our bodies into their likeness as they build up our lives from within.

May our lives be pleasing to the great Banker of the universe so that he will issue us some "celestial letters of credit."

Half-a-Minder

In his book *Enthusiasm Makes the Difference*, Dr. Norman Vincent Peale describes some of those important situations whose good may be made negotiable in other lives. To clearly understand the successes and failures of others teaches us how we can more effectively adjust and adorn our own lives.

Dr. Peale is interested in the fundamental causes of certain human responses, and he has helped a lot of people make their lives more effective by learning from each other. Over the years he has spoken to a large number of conventions of business people. On one of these occasions, after he had gone to his hotel room a woman called him on the telephone. She asked his permission to bring her husband up to his room for a personal interview. Far into the night they all discussed the husband's problems.

It appeared that for a long time this woman had been trying to help her husband to be a little more successful. However, this had not worked very well, and her present attitude indicated that she was about at the end of her rope. Evidently her husband was a fine person, but he had never done very well, either in his business life or in their home, and apparently his wife was about ready to give up. As a kind of last resort she had brought him to see Dr. Peale with a hope that he might be able to help him. She said to Dr. Peale, "I wish you could do something for Charlie."

Dr. Peale found Charlie to be a pleasant, easy-going, likable person, but he had not disciplined himself very well and certainly he was not highly motivated. While he had not done very well in his sales job, his firm had been patient with him, for in spite of his shortcomings, they recognized that he had great potential. Dr. Peale attempted to help by meeting with him at intervals over a few months.

As they got better acquainted, Dr. Peale wrote, he noticed that Charlie continually used one stock phrase. "It was so repetitive that it gave the impression of a phonograph needle stuck in a groove in the record." As each good suggestion was being made, Charlie would say, "You know, I have half a mind to do something about that," or "I have half a mind to investigate that." Dr. Peale said, "Once when I was urging him to think a little more positively, he said, 'You know, I have half a mind to try that.' " Finally, Dr. Peale said to him, "Charlie, I know what's the matter with you. You're a half-a-minder. Everything you think of doing, you have only half a mind to do it."

One of the first requirements for any success is to understand that the human mind is the greatest invention since creation and is capable of any success. However, just half-a-mind is not very effective. To be at one's best, he needs to have a whole mind and to have it all on the job at the same time. It should also be a sound mind and a balanced mind and a positive mind and an enthusiastic mind. Any real accomplishment requires a mind that has been fully made up, fully disciplined, effectively focused, powerfully motivated, and set on fire with a great purpose and a full enthusiasm. When the mind is divided so that it functions only as a fraction, its power is lost. Even an automobile never functions very well when only half of it is in working order. Likewise, even the greatest mind can be corroded by disuse or weakened by indecision. It may lose its balance by wrong thinking, and mental power is soon dissipated when it is not fully disciplined and fully used.

It is an immutable law that when one refuses to use the abilities that God has given him, the abilities are always repossessed. Because the mole didn't use his eyes, nature took away his eyesight. Most people are given a mind that is ample for their needs, but there is none to spare. We are allowed to keep only those abilities that we make good use of. Our mental powers are like the manna that was given to the Israelites in the desert—that which was not used spoiled. However, a whole, fully used, well-disciplined mind is not only our most productive possession, but its abilities can be increased to suit almost any need. Paul said to the Romans, "Be ye transformed by the renewing of your mind" (Romans 12:2).

A regenerated mind with perfected vigor is not only able to transform us, but it can transform everything around us. All that Charlie needed was to get his whole mind on the job and fill it with his chosen purpose. That is generally the same problem that faces most of us. However, we run serious risks when we allow any part of our great natural endowments to lie unused or undisciplined.

A famous Canadian athletic coach once said that most people both in and out of athletics were hold-outs. What he meant was that so frequently we fail to fully invest ourselves in what we are doing. We have too many reservations about things. We go into life with our fingers crossed, so to speak. And when we hold out on life, life holds out on us. Charlie was a hold-out on his own success. He was a hold-out on his wife, and he was a hold-out on God. He was discrediting his Creator by not making the best use of his God-given abilities. Our Creator has a right to have great pride in his creations, and we dishonor God when we commit such serious hold-out sins as fractional devotion and minimum performance. He is not pleased when we practice marginal morals, half-mindedness, and half-heartedness in those important things that life has given us to do. As Dr. Peale would say, "It is our enthusiasm that makes the difference."

In order to make the best and the most of our lives, the law of success requires us to invest our whole minds and our whole souls and our whole selves in our own destiny. No obstacle can for long obstruct the path of a whole-souled, whole-minded, enthusiastic, industrious person.

The human brain is by long odds the finest piece of equipment ever known. It can bring about any success. It has been said that if you want to hatch out something, just set your mind on it. A prominent British neurophysicist said that you could not construct an electronic computer for three billion dollars that would be the equivalent of a human brain. After making that kind of an investment in us, God may get a little bit discouraged at the small return he is getting on his money.

The tragedy of life is that so many of us are only half-minders. Woodrow Wilson once said, "The greatest ability of the American people is their ability to resist instruction." Most of us have our full share of that unfortunate talent. Thomas A. Edison once said, "There is nothing a person will not do to avoid the real effort of thinking." Real thinking is the most unpleasant, disagreeable thing that most of us ever do, and yet Solomon said: "As [a man] thinketh . . . , so is he" (Proverbs 23:7). I am not quite sure just where that situation leaves us, but if we are what we think, and if we don't think, we may be sure that we have a problem.

The human brain is also the greatest problem-solver. It is the most wonderful creator. Out of the brain of Thomas A. Edison came a whole string of inventive creations. Mr. Edison gave us his own formula for success as "99 percent perspiration and 1 percent inspiration."

We now say that Mr. Edison was a natural-born success, but he was kicked out of school when he was fourteen because it was thought he was too dumb to learn. However, Mr. Edison disciplined his mind and kept it fully focused until it learned to do whatever he assigned to it. Because Edison was whole-hearted and whole-minded, his actual accomplishment approached his potential about as nearly as possible. His secret was that each time he used his mind effectively, its powers increased. Our minds are also capable of producing all the attitudes, skills, habits, abilities, and know-how necessary to make our lives outstanding.

The world's greatest literature, as well as its greatest financial successes and scientific miracles, all came from human brains. Someone has said: "I love to lose myself in other men's minds. I love the minds of men, and I love the men who use their minds." A good mind always has a well-developed set of ambitions, and it has usually been definitely "made up" on all of the important issues with which it is involved. The mind is that part of us that perceives, wills, thinks, decides, solves, resolves, remembers, dreams, reasons, and motivates. It determines moods, regulates dispositions, forms attitudes, creates enthusiasms, and incites desires. But think of the waste when someone becomes a half-a-minder.

The scripture speaks of a related condition when it says "a double minded man is unstable in all his ways" (James 1:8). Actually, a double-minded man is only half-a-minder. When one has two things in his mind there can't be more than half a mind for each, but a double mind also loses its focus and its strength as well as its stability.

A certain prizefighter was once badly defeated in the fight ring. After the bout was over, one of his friends was rubbing him with liniment and trying to encourage him by doing a little commiserating. He said to the fighter: "You really did get a pretty bad licking, didn't you?" The fighter said: "Yes, I did, but I now know where I made my mistake; I should have knocked him out in the first round when he was alone."

When any prizefighter procrastinates his success until knocks on his head fill the ring with several phantom opponents, his job becomes much more complicated. In life we also have trouble with a distorted, multiple vision, which makes us unable to tell which of our opponents are the real ones. The writer of Ecclesiastes gave us a good idea for avoiding the confusions of life when, in concluding his book, he said: "Let us hear the conclusion of the whole matter: Fear God, and keep his commandments: for this is the whole duty of man" (Ecclesiastes 12:13).

Jesus gave an excellent expression about the weakness caused by our double exposures when he said, "No man can serve two masters" (Matthew 6:24). It is pretty difficult to ride two horses in the same race. We heard of a man who tried that once, and just as he was getting everything going to his liking, the horses ran on opposite sides of a tree.

With a double vision, we get involved in too many conflicts of interest in which we are fighting ourselves. When one tries to ride two horses or maintain two loyalties or foster two ideologies, he makes himself a half-a-minder. Jesus pointed out that no one could serve God and mammon. One can't look up and down simultaneously; one can't move forward and backward at the same time.

There is one primary purpose for our lives upon this earth and that is to work out our eternal salvation. If we fail in this main objective, then nothing else will ever be of much consequence. The scripture says, "Whatsoever thy hand findeth to do, do it with thy might" (Ecclesiastes 9:10). That means to be whole-minded and whole-hearted.

In one of his greatest success pronouncements, the Master said: "Therefore, O ye that embark in the service of God, see that ye serve him with all your heart, might, mind and strength, that ye may stand blameless before God at the last day" (D&C 4:2). The great secret of success in life is to coordinate all our powers into one cooperative effort involving a joint action of the heart, the mind, the might, and the physical strength.

How do we serve God with our heart? That requires a whole-souled devotion. We can serve him with a full love and an undivided worship. How do we serve God with our mind? That is done through our ability to study, to think, to reason, and to understand. To serve God with our mind requires a positive mental attitude and an ability to build up a righteous enthusiasm. How do we serve God with our might? That is our physical activity. We are judged according to our works. Then when we get all of these powers coordinated and harnessed, we get success.

Christianity itself is not just a set of ideas; it is a set of coordinated activities. Even faith dies when the works are taken away. Faith has little value by itself. However, by this process of consolidation and joint action, one may make himself whole. He may concentrate all of the elements of personal power into one determined effort. He thereby achieves a wholehearted centrality in his purpose. His effort becomes concentrated, highly focused, and all in one piece, rather than being merely a jumble of many-directioned impulses held loosely together by circumstances. sometimes we take too much pride in merely knowing that the gospel is true. Satan knows that the gospel is true, but instead of that knowledge helping him, it actually hurts him; whereas the mark of a true follower of Christ is that he fully lives those principles he believes in. The proverb says: "Wherever thou art, be wholly there."

Jan Smuts, the great South African prime minister, once said that the greatest of all sins is fragmentation, whereas the greatest virtue is "wholeism." The great word *holy* came from the word *whole,* and it means to be complete. It would be pretty hard for anyone to be whole or holy while he was half-minded or half-hearted or half-righteous.

We speak of God as being holy. That is because he is whole. He is complete. He is all-wise. He has all knowledge and all power. He is all-good. In him there is no darkness, no sin, no indecision, no ignorance, and no indifference. The objective of our lives is that we may someday be holy also. However, before we can be whole, our spirits and our bodies must be inseparably joined together in the resurrection. We must transform our minds by getting rid of our sins and weaknesses. Then we will no longer have half a mind, because to be sinful or to be half-a-minder is also to be weak. Above all other things we need to foster our ambition to be whole, to be complete, and to be as God is.

No Man Is an Island

Ernest Hemingway wrote a best seller under the title *For Whom the Bell Tolls.* The setting of the book is the Spanish Civil War of the middle 1930s. The title was taken from John Donne's famous statement, in which he says:

> No man is an island, entire of itself; every man is a piece of the continent, a part of the main; if a clod be washed away by the sea, Europe is the less, as well as if a promontory were, as well as if a manor of thy friends or of thine own were; any man's death diminishes me, because I am involved in mankind: and therefore never send to know for whom the bell tolls; it tolls for thee.

Every man has a stake in every other man's accomplishment. Each man holds an interest in every man's deeds. When someone beautifies the landscape or invents a labor-saving device, all are enriched. When the tide comes in, all of the ships in the harbor are lifted up. When someone improves the frontiers of his own mind or spirit, the general intellectual or spiritual level is raised. Likewise, when anyone dies we are diminished, for a part of us has also passed away. Therefore, who can ask for whom the bell tolls? It tolls for the dead, but it tolls for all. "It tolls for thee."

No one lives unto himself alone and no one dies unto himself alone. Life is not a game of solitaire. The whole community, the whole church, the whole nation are involved in every individual in it. If the shortstop makes an error in a baseball game, the whole team may lose. If one football player is offside, all of his associates are penalized. If the garbage in one household is not collected, the whole community may be a victim of disease. If my little finger is infected, I cannot laugh it off because it is just my *little* finger. By itself one finger may be little and unimportant, but the infection even in my smallest finger places my whole body in jeopardy.

There is a blood stream biological, but there is also a blood stream sociological. There is a blood stream spiritual, and there is a blood stream financial. It is far better judgment to help purify the general supply than to permit poison to remain in even the most unimportant of its parts.

It is incorrect for a person to say about the tragedy of another, "That's *his* funeral," because it is also ours. We dare not ignore the needs of others, whether it be for their bodies, their minds, their souls, or their pocketbooks, because we are more or less all in the same boat.

It was once reported that two Irishmen were coming to America in an ocean liner. One rushed up to the other and shouted, "The ship is sinking." The other Irishman shouted back, "Let 'er sink, she ain't our'n." When capital and labor have a common source of benefits, one cannot say to the other, "Let 'er sink, she ain't our'n." The Sunday School cannot say of the Relief Society "Let 'er sink, she ain't our'n." Paul expressed this idea with the thought that no part of the body can say to any other, "I have no need of thee" (1 Corinthians 12:21). All are important. It is very necessary that we understand and master this philosophy as it applies in every field.

For example, in becoming a millionaire Andrew Carnegie made thirty-eight other men millionaires. As he became successful he enriched his suppliers, his associates, and all with whom he did business. Likewise, when someone "goes broke," he tends to drag everyone else down. His employees lose their jobs, his suppliers lose their business, his creditors lose their money. They may also lose their good example, their fountain of inspiration, and their source of good ideas.

This idea is in continuous operation in education and in all of our social and religious relationships. It applies to us educationally, morally, spiritually, and financially. To glory in every man's accomplishment is just good sense, because each individual success helps to recast the general welfare on a higher level. An increase in leadership ability or in the spiritual effectiveness of others not only makes us more capable but also makes us better men. Men, like planets, have orbits, and it is the attraction of the others that holds us in place.

In America we all benefit from the general good. As doctors in any part of the country become more skilled, the health of all people is improved and made more secure. The general success is our gain. We tend to absorb the education, culture, and integrity of those among whom we live.

That is particularly true in the Church. Most of the benefits of our lives we have received from others. We absorb their inspiration and receive courage from their example. When our associates reach new levels of faith they draw us upward, just as any athlete is always made better when he plays on a winning team. It is said that when anyone puts on the uniform of the New York Yankees, his baseball ability always jumps a few points. That is also true of one working in a church group with high standards. No one ever reaches his greatest accomplishment alone. There are no one-man teams in the Church. There are no one-man teams in success. In either case no man is an island. No family is an island. No nation is an island. We all depend on each other.

An Iowa farmer won many national championships year after year for growing the best seed corn. Every year as he developed a better strain of corn he shared his improved seed with his neighbors. A newspaper man thought this procedure very strange and asked the farmer why he helped those who might be his most serious competitors. The farmer explained that if he allowed his neighbors to grow poor corn, the bees and the wind would carry the pollen from their fields and pollinate his crop. Therefore, the better his neighbor's corn, the greater his chances would be to win the championship.

There is a far more important cross-pollination taking place in ideas and ideals among us than in the seed corn of any Iowa farmer. No one can uplift someone else without himself being made better. It is a natural law that the teacher always learns more than the student. Just "Tow your brother's boat across, and lo, your own has reached the shore."

> For life is a mirror of king and slave—
> Tis just what you are and do;
> Then give to the world the best you have,
> And the best will come back to you.

Occasionally there are some misguided unfortunates who, for one reason or another, try to sow seeds of discontent and discouragement among others. They think the way to lift themselves up is to pull others down. But almost always when a person digs a pit for someone else he is the one that falls into it.

It does not add to the general security for any apple in the barrel to develop a rotten spot. Rottenness spreads quickly among apples and people, and no one can tell where it will end. Dealing in rottenness is like dealing in any other disease. The one who is in closest contact with the disease is the one who finds the most difficulty in escaping from it.

When anyone lives at less than his best, a general downdraft is started which affects all within range. Everyone is a carrier of something. To be within the contamination range of sinful, careless people is to run the risk of becoming like them, and it is far easier to cure one who has been poisoned in his blood than in his principles.

In composing the Declaration of Independence, Thomas Jefferson wrote, "For the support of this Declaration . . . we mutually pledge to each other our Lives, our Fortunes and our sacred Honor." To support others is not only our responsibility, it is also our greatest opportunity, for we are all in the same boat. In one sense we all rise or fall, sink or swim together. We share in every man's success, we live a part of every man's life, and we die a part of every man's death. A common need, a common interest, and a common destiny bind us together. This applies even beyond mortality. The Prophet Joseph Smith informed us that if we don't seek out our dead and do what we can in their interests we imperil our own salvation. The Prophet Malachi said that if children's hearts were not turned to their fathers and vice versa, the whole earth would be smitten with a curse. Such a philosophy for here and hereafter gives us a great personal interest in the concept so eloquently expressed by John Donne that no man is an island.

The Idea Bank

One of the most important businesses in the world is the banking business. A bank is a place in which we keep things safe for future use. We have money banks; we have blood banks; we have soil banks. And it has been suggested that everyone ought to have an idea bank.

One of the reasons why we have banks to put our money in is to keep it from slipping through our fingers and getting lost. That is exactly the reason for an idea bank. The pocket is not a very suitable place to keep valuable possessions, nor is the head a very good place to keep ideas. In the first place, the brain was never intended as a warehouse; it is a workroom. The brain does not serve very well as an idea bank because it is so full of leaks. Ideas in the brain are like water in a leaky cask. Just try holding a lot of ideas in your mind over a long period and see what happens.

One of our difficulties is that the forgetting process is an unconscious process. The moment of learning is a conscious moment, but that of forgetting is unconscious. It is like the moment of birth. Presumably we never know that we are being born until some time after it has happened. It is like that with forgetting. We are not conscious of the thoughts that are slipping away from us, and therefore we fail to take adequate precautions against their loss. For a great many people old ideas are being lost far more rapidly than new ones are being acquired. We can easily figure out where this will lead us.

The scriptures suggest that we should have a "book of remembrance" to help us keep track of important matters. When the Lord visited John the Revelator on the Isle of Patmos he indicated the importance of preserving ideas. He said, "Write the things which thou hast seen, and the things which are, and the things which shall be hereafter" (Revelation 1:19). By writing an idea down, we can keep it forever in all of its youthful bloom and impressiveness of meaning. Just think what a tragedy it would have been if John had tried to keep the book of Revelation in his head instead of putting it down on paper!

When the Lord was giving the great revelation to Joseph Smith and Sidney Rigdon recorded in section 76 of the Doctrine and Covenants, he told them four times to write down the things they had seen and heard. In verse 28 is recorded the following: "And while we were yet in the Spirit, the Lord commanded us that we should write the vision." Substantially the same admonition was given again in verses 49, 80, and 113. And three of the four times the Lord said it should be written down while they were "yet in the Spirit."

The Lord had a good reason for this. Words quickly slip through the memory; impressions fade; ideas lose their meaning and impressiveness with the passage of time. One way to avoid losing our money is to hurry and put it in the bank while we still have it. A good way to avoid losing ideas is to write them down while they are fresh and we are "yet in the Spirit." Great men have always been bankers of ideas. Hawthorne's notebooks show that he never let a significant thought or circumstance escape his pen. Robert Louis Stevenson always carried with him two books: one to read from and one to write in. It is told that during an important interview, Goethe suddenly excused himself and went into an adjoining room, where he wrote down for his *Faust* a thought he had just received, lest it should be forgotten before the interview was over.

Soon after Alma was made the chief judge of his people he inquired of the Lord what he should do concerning certain matters. The Lord gave him the necessary instructions, and the record says, "And it came to pass when Alma had heard these words, he wrote them down so that he might have them" (Mosiah 27:33). Alma knew that his memory was not to be trusted even with the words of the Lord, so he simply wrote them down to preserve them not only for himself but for us also.

The Lord commanded the brother of Jared to write the things he had shown him (Ether 4:1). At the time of the Lord's visit to the Nephites after his resurrection, he said, "I command you that ye shall write these sayings" (3 Nephi 16:4). This repetition emphasizes the fact that ideas are perishable and extremely valuable. In fact, one of the most important differences in people is found in the number and quality of their ideas. The difference between Saul of Tarsus before and after his conversion was in the way his ideas had changed. Thomas A. Edison was different from most other people because of the nature and quality of his ideas.

There are certain ideas that can be of particular value to us. They may be in prose or verse or song, but if we get the right ones and then really get them into our system, they will inspire, instruct, and charm us. Just as certain kinds of food vitalize and build us up, so everyone has natural sympathies for and susceptibilities to ideas. Certain musical renditions have great power to arouse the enthusiasm of some people and set their accomplishment in motion. There are ideas like that. They may be our own ideas, or they may belong to someone else. Our own ideas sometimes fit into our own mental and emotional machinery a little better than do the ideas of others, yet even our own ideas are subject to a terrible shrinkage if we don't bank them in a safe place.

Idea stimulants in the form of poems, bits of philosophy, or quotations have the ability to stir us up and develop our enthusiasm and our faith. We ought to memorize not only the words of the ideas but the spirit as well. This will help us bring our accomplishment to its highest point. But in addition, we ought to make sure that we also have these precious gems of thought in the bank for permanent safekeeping. There are particular quotations from other people that serve a special need in us. We should get possession of these ideas that have a peculiar affinity for our minds and put them in the bank where they can be adapted and harnessed to do our work.

The fact that an idea may have belonged to someone else originally does not lessen its value to us. Most of us do not write our own music or paint our own pictures, yet they play a constructive role in our lives. The scriptures have been put into words by other people, yet we use them for our own uplift. Emerson says that next to him who first expresses a great truth is he who quotes it. He might have said that he who *lives* a great truth is even ahead of him who first expresses it.

Suppose, then, that we get some kind of idea file and earnestly go into the business of banking ideas. The repository itself may be a set of folders or it may be an 8½-by 11-inch looseleaf binder with a good quality of paper, where we can write and paste or otherwise deposit our ideas in a permanent collection. This will preserve the vividness and power of a mental impression, for otherwise it fades with time. The rate of fading is not uniform. One section of a thought may completely drop from view in an instant; with another the rate of loss is more gradual. But in any event, our lives are poorer as a consequence of every loss. A good file and a poor memory are a far better combination than a good memory and a poor file. Therefore, one of the first investments that every aspiring leader, teacher, or reader should make is in a pair of scissors and a pot of glue.

A person may have great learning but "miss the boat" because he has "little remembering." People may acquire the equivalent of several college educations during a lifetime but never have more than a smattering of education on hand at any one time. We often reach a plateau early in life from which we never rise substantially, because our forgetting processes become more active than our learning processes.

Significant words and thoughts are not intended to be used just once but many times. You would not listen to a stirring piece of music just once and then throw away the recording, nor would you just take one look at a beautiful painting and then discard it. Rather, you would try to get possession of it so that it could uplift you many times. Great ideas can serve us again and again to instruct and inspire our minds.

One great man says that when he wants to give himself a lift, he always turns to these selected ideas, some of which he has written himself. They are like his own children or his trusted friends. The people we call friends have more power to lift us up and give us pleasure. But there are also ideas that are particularly friendly to us personally. It is a great tragedy to lose a friend, and yet a fortune is lost every day in friendly, helpful ideas, simply because we have no banking system and have not formed the right banking habits.

Ideas often earn a far greater rate of interest than money in the bank. But we must first capture and learn to control them. This requires skill. Sometimes ideas come in flashes of inspiration; they sometimes hesitate in our minds for only an instant and then, like a bird that lights for a moment in a tree, they are gone. Ideas sometimes come in chains of thought. Sometimes they come in clusters or family groups. They sometimes form a phalanx that pounds and forces it way, pushing everything else out of our minds. Sometimes we have thoughts of optimism, courage, and devotion, thoughts capable of changing our lives. A certain kind of idea in the mind sends a tingle through the emotions and quickens the whole personality. Thoughts are carriers of ambition and power. They can rejuvenate us and put us on our feet with a new lease on life.

These thoughts should be written down while we are "yet in the spirit." For ideas furnish the substance out of which life and successful leadership are made. When we lose a good idea we have lost a part of ourselves. When we add the right kind of thoughts we have increased our life's volume. We should make them our permanent property so that we can control them. We can acquire them originally under a sort of homestead act by putting a fence around them and settling on them long enough to get a permanent title.

Suppose you went to a great conference, a banquet of ideas, that lasted for a week. It was a thrilling experience for you. Suppose that during this five-day period you received fifty really worthwhile ideas. But the only receptacle you had in which to store these ideas was your head. Even before the conference was over, 50 percent of these valuable possessions would already have passed beyond recall. In six months, 80 percent would have slipped through the fingers of your mind. Two years later 99 percent would have been lost.

If ideas are not valuable, why spend valuable time acquiring them? If they are valuable, why not take steps to retain them? Sir Henry Sidney said: "If you hear a wise sentence or an apt phrase, write it down." It will then form associations with other ideas in your mind to build the unity that gives strength. It has been said that one reason why ideas die so quickly in some heads is that they can't stand solitary confinement. "Quotable quotes" are not more valuable than your own "notable quotes." Montaigne said, "I quote others the better to express myself."

When ideas are first received in the mind they are likely to feel insecure. They have not yet established a well-developed root system. If they are reviewed and thought about frequently they will in time securely establish themselves.

It is a great sight to see a bank with the shelves loaded with money. It is a greater sight to see an idea bank with the shelves loaded with inspiration, power, and know-how. Making money loses much of its significance if we don't save some of what we make. And money that is put in the bank earns more interest than does that which is kept in the pocket. Don't worry if you haven't much to save at first. Once you get the habit, the amounts will increase rapidly. It is also true that ideas can soon grow into a surprisingly large estate.

Sometimes we use the word *impression* in speaking of a thought we have just received. The word is an apt one. Receiving a thought is like making a scratch on the surface of the mind. The deeper it is cut, the longer it will last.

Ideas and ideals, like everything else, are born small. Little babies cannot work as hard as grown-ups. So a baby thought, newly arrived in your mind, needs to be cared for and carefully brought to maturity.

Early-day civilization was plagued with a very high rate of

infant mortality. We should see to it that our life is not plagued by an excessive rate of infant mortality among our ideas, ideals, and leadership traits. The one procedure that will reduce this waste is to have the mind get hold of as many good ideas as it can and then write them down while we are "yet in the spirit." Then we will be in the banking business in the most profitable meaning of the phrase.

The Fall of Man

Some time ago I heard a radio speaker discussing the fall of Adam. He seemed to think Adam should be held responsible for most of the troubles that are presently plaguing our world. He was greatly disturbed that the patriarch of the race should have inflicted so many woes upon an innocent posterity.

This old sectarian doctrine, built around the idea of man's natural depravity and weakness inherited from Adam, is at the root of innumerable problems among us. In the first place, this doctrine is entirely untrue. Adam was one of the greatest men who has ever lived upon the earth. In the premortal councils in heaven before the earth was created, Adam was Michael, the archangel, who under Jehovah led the hosts of heaven against Lucifer. Because of his merit as one of the greatest intelligences of heaven, he was chosen to be our earthly progenitor and the patriarch of the family of God upon the earth.

John the Revelator tells us: "And there was war in heaven: Michael and his angels fought against the dragon; and the dragon fought and his angels, And prevailed not; neither was their place found any more in heaven. And the great dragon was cast out . . . into the earth, and his angels were cast out with him." (Revelation 12:9.) That is, before Adam was born, God had decreed that Satan should be in the world, where through the law of opposites men would have a chance to choose between good and evil.

The opportunity to sin is in the world because it is a part of the program of man's testing and developing. God could destroy sin. He could also destroy Satan at any instant he desired. Then we might ask, Why doesn't he? He himself has given us the answer. He has said: "And it must needs be that the devil should tempt the children of men, or they could not be agents unto themselves: for if they never should have bitter they could not know the sweet" (D&C 29:39). God has unalterably committed himself to the principle of our free agency.

The fall of Adam had been foreknown and an atonement provided even before the earth was formed. Peter said, "Ye were not redeemed with corruptible things, as silver and gold . . . but with the precious blood of Christ, as of a lamb without blemish . . . who verily was foreordained before the foundation of the world." (1 Peter 1:18-20.)

If sin was to be in the world as an accepted part of the divine plan, then it was appropriate that man himself should introduce it. God had said to Adam, "Of the tree of the knowledge of good and evil, thou shall not eat of it, nevertheless, thou mayest choose for thyself" (Moses 3:17).

After Eve had been deceived and had eaten, Adam made his own choice, as God had already given him leave. As Paul says, "Adam was not deceived, but the woman being deceived was in the transgression" (1 Timothy 2:14). After they had partaken, God said, "The man is become as one of us to know good and evil" (Moses 4:28). That does not sound like weakness or depravity.

Adam knew what he was doing and acted wisely in our interests. Modern revelation tells us that Adam rejoiced in what he had done, and said, "Blessed be the name of God, for because of my transgression my eyes are opened, and in this life I shall have joy, and again in the flesh I shall see God." Mother Eve joined with her husband in this rejoicing: "Were it not for our transgression we never should have had seed, and never should have known good and evil, and the joy of our redemption, and the eternal life which God giveth unto all the obedient." (Moses 5:10, 11.) Knowing the scriptures, no one could wish that Adam and Eve had done differently than they did.

Adam fell, but he fell in the right direction. He fell toward the goal. He made possible many blessings that we would not otherwise have had. If there had been no fall, there would have been no atonement, and no atonement would have meant no Savior.

The fall of Adam was not a sexual sin, as had been supposed by some. Adam and Eve were married by the Lord himself before sin ever entered the world. The Fall came because they took into their bodies something that brought about their mortality and therefore ultimate death. But it was ordained of God in advance of this life that men should die, and our redemption and resurrection had also been provided for. Paul said, "For as in Adam all die, even so in Christ shall all be made alive" (1 Corinthians 15:22). But we were not cheated by what Adam did, and we have the sure word of the Lord that we will be punished only for our *own* sins and not for Adam's transgression. The fall of man was a blessing in many ways, and like many of our blessings, it came in disguise.

Lehi told his son Jacob:

> And now, behold, if Adam had not transgressed he would not have fallen, but he would have remained in the garden of Eden. . . .
>
> And they would have had no children; wherefore they would have remained in a state of innocence, having no joy, for they knew no misery; doing no good, for they knew no sin.
>
> But behold, all things have been done in the wisdom of him who knoweth all things.
>
> Adam fell that men might be, and men are that they might have joy. (2 Nephi 2:22–25.)

We have every reason to be very proud of the great patriarch of our race. Father Adam was not a big-time scallywag, as some people actually seem to think, nor was he an evolutionary missing link standing on some low level between man and some lesser form of life. Adam was high in the ruling councils of heaven in his first estate, and he was faithful and true throughout his 930 years of mortality.

Three years before the death of Adam, he called his righteous posterity together in the valley of Adam-ondi-Ahman and there bestowed upon them his last blessing. And the Lord appeared to them, and the people rose up and blessed Adam and called him Michael, the prince, the archangel.

> And the Lord administered comfort unto Adam, and said unto him: I have set thee to be at the head; a multitude of nations shall come of thee, and thou art a prince over them forever.
>
> And Adam stood up in the midst of the congregation; and, notwithstanding he was bowed down with age, being full of the Holy Ghost, predicted whatsoever should befall his posterity unto the latest generation. (D&C 107:55–56.)

Under Christ, Adam still stands at the head of this great family of earth, and he will have an important part in our future lives. The Prophet Daniel said: "I beheld till the thrones were cast down, and the Ancient of days did sit, whose garment was white as snow, and the hair of his head like the pure wool: his throne was like the fiery flame, and his wheels as burning fire" (Daniel 7:9). The Ancient of days Daniel referred to is Adam.

But in a little different sense the fall of man was not something that was finished and done with in the Garden of Eden six thousand years ago. A far more destructive version of the fall of man is now going on, and those who take part in it must themselves bear the punishment. Anyone who will just put his ear to the ground at any hour of the day or night will hear the steady thud, thud, thud of the fall of man. Each new day we have new Sabbath breakers, new profanity users, new adulterers, and new violators of every one of God's laws. Daily there are new people falling into the cesspools of sin and the mud puddles of human delinquency and error. The jails, the reform schools, and the mental hospitals are being filled to overflowing by this treacherous downward movement. New lives are being spoiled, new homes are being broken up, and many new footprints are being made on the broad road that leads to death. *Adam* fell upward, but much of the present motion of his posterity is in the other direction.

There is an editor of a religious magazine who conducts a column attempting to help people with their troubles. He received a letter from a fifteen-year-old girl as follows: "I am one of eleven members in my family. We all serve God except my father; please pray for him." A mother wrote: "Please pray for my husband, who is an alcoholic." Another mother said: "I married a man who resembles a human being in shape and appearance only. After a siege of threats and violence which would be hard for anyone to believe, he left me without a cent with four children. But not before my oldest girl was driven to suicide because of him. The state has taken my three other children. The court tore my five-year-old boy away from me, and I can still hear his screams for me to help him. Please pray for us."

The editor says that these pleas are fairly representative of many letters received. Such requests reflect the heartbreak, discouragement, sorrow, and desperation that many people face throughout the world. And almost every defeat, broken heart, nervous breakdown, divorce, violence, alcoholism and case of suffering came about because someone transgressed the word of the Lord, bringing on this modern-day fall of man. This devastating wave of sin is not something that took place only among the earliest inhabitants of the earth. This is what is going on in Christian America in the greatest age of enlightenment and with the highest standard of living and education ever known in the world.

Man was created in the image of God and was given dominion over all the earth, but he has failed to get dominion over his own appetites and sinful temptations, therefore he is falling from the high place intended for him by the Creator. The fall most often takes place just a little bit at a time. We sin in just little things at first. We take a few privileges with our conscience. We take a few nibbles at unrighteousness, and we fall correspondingly.

In his great epic poem *Paradise Lost,* John Milton pictures Satan as falling nine days and nights to finally land in hell. Many of us fall at a slower rate, but for a much longer period. But the landing place may be the same. We are all familiar with the physical law that tends to pull things toward the earth, but this ancient law of attraction is not restricted in its operation to a world of substance. There a spiritual gravity. As we relax our hold on righteousness and on the word of the Lord, we soon sink to a lower level of values.

A life that isn't being constantly improved slips downward. It takes constant steering to keep the car of life on the road. You can't lash the steering wheel fast and avoid a crack-up. Christianity is not just a set of ideas, it is also a set of activities. If firmly held onto, they will prevent our spiritual downfall and death.

A little boy once fell out of bed, and when someone asked him how it happened he said, "I suppose I went to sleep too close to where I got in." In our religious lives we sometimes fall asleep too near the edge. We need to get further into religion, and we need to get religion further into us. Then we may be able to walk a little more securely among life's temptations without causing this tragic thud, thud, thud of our own downfall. Like the little boy, most of us "fall" in our sleep. Only eternal vigilance is the price of safety.

Jesus pointed out our greatest need when he said, "Come up higher." We need to raise the standard of our thinking as well as of our living. We need to fill our hearts with righteousness and practice the gospel of fairness, honesty, and responsibility. Only by this means can we stop the destructive downward tendency so common in the life of man.

Jack the Giant-Killer

Some time ago I reread that very interesting old English folktale, "Jack the Giant-Killer." It recounts how, in the days of King Arthur, a giant by the name of Cormoran lived on Cornwall Island, a short distance beyond Land's End. Cormoran frequently indulged in a very bad habit of wading across the intervening bit of sea, frightening the people out of their villages, and then loading himself up with their cattle and sheep to carry back to his island.

Living in the village was a young farmer boy whose name was Jack. Jack was a very resourceful, thoughtful young man, and one day he asked his father why something wasn't done about Cormoran. Jack's father explained that Cormoran was a giant and even King Arthur's knights sought no fights with giants.

But Jack told his father that his teacher had explained to him that there was a solution to every problem, and Jack said he believed there was a solution to the problem of Cormoran and he intended to find it.

A few nights later Jack put an ax, a pick, and a shovel into his boat and rowed out to the island where the giant lived. While Cormoran was asleep Jack dug a deep pit in front of the cave where Cormoran slept. Then just before dawn Jack sent a loud blast from his horn through the cave. The giant was very angry, and roaring with rage and uttering threats of vengeance, he stumbled out through the darkness and fell into the hole. Jack was on hand with his ax and gave the giant a good sound thump on the head that was hard enough to solve forever the problem of Cormoran.

When the people living in the next county heard that Jack had killed the giant, they immediately invited him to come and perform a like service for the giant that was troubling them. When Jack got there he found that their giant had two heads, and this required a little different handling. But Jack knew that there was a solution to every problem, and all he needed to do was to find the right answer.

Jack's success at solving giant problems was soon noised around, and other requests began coming in, but every giant problem required a different answer. Some of these giants had eyes in the backs of their heads. One had a magic coat that made him invisible. One had a magic cap which enabled him to learn things no one else knew. One had a magic sword that could cut through the strongest iron. One had a pair of magic shoes that gave him extraordinary swiftness. But Jack knew that there was a solution to every problem, and when the right solution was supported with sufficient skill, courage, and industry, every problem could be solved. Finally he was given the highly complimentary title of Jack the Giant-Killer.

This is far more than just a very interesting story. It is also a most worthwhile philosophy of life. Our worst difficulties arise because of our inability to solve our problems properly. As one example, we see the giant nations roaring and snarling at each other and threatening to destroy the world and everyone in it because they can't solve a problem. Think what a wonderful world we could have if all the great nations would stop creating problems and develop a little greater ability as problem solvers. That might also serve as one of the primary objectives for our own individual accomplishment.

We should, of course, keep in mind that not all of our problems come from giants. The most tiny problems are often too much for some of us to solve. We frequently fail because we spend so much time worrying about the problem that we have no time left to work out good solutions.

We might get some helpful ideas from a famous problem

solver of the Old Testament by the name of David. David could not go into the army as his brothers did because he was too young, so he stayed at home and looked after the family sheep. But one day Father Jesse sent David to King Saul's camp to take his brothers some food. When he arrived, the camp was a scene of great confusion. A giant from Gath by the name of Goliath was challenging Saul's soldiers to choose a champion from among them to fight Goliath and decide the war by a single combat. Everyone in Saul's camp was desperately scared. In their fear no one was thinking about solutions, and it looked as though they would all soon be slaves to the Philistines.

But David had had some experience as a problem solver. When a lion and a bear had come among his sheep, he didn't run and hide, but solved the problem by killing the lion and the bear. Seeing now the confusion and the helplessness of the Israelites, David set out to help them with their problem.

To King Saul he said, "Let no man's heart fail because of [Goliath], for thy servant will go and fight with this Philistine." Saul pointed out the danger and called attention to the fact that David was a very young man, whereas Goliath was not only a giant, he was also the champion warrior among all the Philistines. Goliath was clad in a coat of mail and carried a spear like a weaver's beam. But David did not abandon himself to fear as the others had done. He said to Saul, "This uncircumcised Philistine shall be to me as [the lion and the bear], seeing he hath defied the armies of the living God."

Saul put his armor on David, but David said, "I cannot go with these, for I have not proved them." Having taken off the armor, he left carrying his staff. On the way he picked up five smooth stones from the brook, and armed with these and his slingshot he went out to meet the giant.

Goliath was a little surprised that his challenge had been accepted by one so young, and he began to threaten and abuse the shepherd boy. But David said to the Philistine, "Thou comest to me with a sword, and with a spear, and with a shield: but I come to thee in the name of . . . the God of the armies of Israel, whom thou hast defied. This day will the Lord deliver thee into mine hand."

I suppose that is what you could call the faith that moves mountains, or at least the faith that kills giants. But David also had a practical program. He put a rock in his slingshot, and as he whirled it to get up momentum, he ran to meet the Philistine. Just at the right time and in the right way, he let the rock go, and it crashed into the forehead of Goliath. The giant fell forward on his face, and David finished the job by cutting off Goliath's head with his own sword. The record says, "And when the Philistines saw their champion was dead, they fled." (1 Samuel 17.)

Having solved the problem, David went back to the sheep. In passing it is interesting to remember that David had used his slingshot before. Unlike Saul's armor, the sling had been proven; and David knew how to put enough steam behind a rock that the Israelite problem of Goliath would stay solved for a long time.

One of the great lessons of the Bible is found in this story of David, the giant-killer, and this is one of those lessons that we most need to learn. In our day we are not bothered with many physical giants who steal our cattle, or threaten us with a sword like a weaver's beam; but just the same, there are a lot of giants that need to be slain. Like Saul's soldiers, we have a choice between being giant-killers or being their slaves, for we are placed in servitude to every problem that we do not overcome.

Therefore, let's think of ourselves as "problem solvers" and work out some solutions to the giant fears that are giving us so much trouble and are robbing us of so much of our success and happiness. There are also some giant discouragements that are annihilating our industry and self-confidence. There are some giant doubts that are destroying our faith in God. Some of our bad habits have attained giant status and are threatening us with a life of serving evil. What we need are the courage and skill to be a giant-killer. Too many Cormorans that should have been gotten rid of long ago are still getting fat at our expense.

An interesting thing about this situation is that everyone must kill his own giants. Certainly one of the most profitable of all undertakings is to develop our skill as problem solvers, for we know that when we overcome the giant of discouragement, our own strength is immediately increased. But if by faith and study we destroy our doubts and settle our confusions, then our strength is multiplied.

One of the best ways to improve our ability as problem solvers is to think more about the solution and spend less time wallowing around in the problem. A fine middle-aged couple came to see me about a marital problem. To begin with they had selected each other from among all the people in the world, yet they couldn't get along together. They both maintained that they wanted to save their marriage. They had no other heart interests, but they seemed to dearly love to point out each other's short-comings, though neither seemed to do very much about them.

One of the husband's complaints was that his wife had invited her mother to live with them. He said he didn't think that was fair. I asked him how long his mother-in-law had been in their home. His wife spoke up and said her mother had died more than eight years previously. I was impressed that almost anyone could figure out a solution to their problem, but that no matter how good the solution was, they would not be able to follow it because they were more interested in fixing the blame and having a fight than in making each other happy. They insisted on wading around in the mud puddle of their problem rather than in cleaning themselves up with an answer. They had created their own giant Cormoran, who was robbing them of love, happiness, and success.

I gave them each a couple of sheets of paper and asked them to do some homework by writing out a clear-cut statement of their problem, putting down on paper as many solutions as they could think of, and bringing their papers back to me in a week. It is an interesting fact that there are always several solutions to every problem. There may not be several successful solutions or even several completely satisfactory solutions, but it develops a person's problem-solving ability to make his canvass of the alter-natives as complete as possible, and then be able expertly and objectively to evaluate and weigh the advantages and disadvantages of each.

The trouble with Saul's soldiers was that they could only think of one way to kill a giant; and that was the impossible way of running a sword or a spear through his heavy armor. David found a spot that had no armor at all, and he also thought of a better way to do the job. David had already developed the skill with a slingshot that would enable him to put his plan into successful operation.

Many people live lives of desperation and confusion because they devote themselves to the problems instead of the answers. Because of this defect in procedure some people can't solve even the most tiny problems. For example, some intelligent people spend a lot of time worrying about occupational success, when they can't get the beds off their backs in the morning. They can't kill inertia, sloth, lethargy, or indifference even in themselves. Isn't it interesting that some people spend their entire lives and never learn how to get up on time in the morning? Try as they may, many can't get rid of the bad habits of caffeine, nicotine, alcohol, or overweight. We consent to be the slaves of negative thinking, evil speaking, profanity, and disbelief rather than develop a plan for digging a trap in front of their caves to enable us to solve the problems.

We read in the Bible about people who were possessed of devils. But is one much better off who puts himself in the clutches of an unsolved problem, and permits himself to be the slave of evil, being forever tormented by some demon that he himself has created?

For many years Peter Marshall was a chaplain in the United States Senate. He prayed, "Lord, help us to be a part of the answer, not a part of the problem." Sometimes we make a quicksand quagmire out of a problem, and then the more we struggle and accuse and fight, the deeper we sink into the difficulty.

One of the worst enemies of solutions is postponement. In the confessions of St. Augustine he pictures himself as a flagrantly worldly and licentious young man. He confessed that the prayer of his wild, youthful days was, "Oh God, give me chastity and self-control, but not just yet."

Referring to the Indians, Brigham Young once said, "It is better to feed them than to fight them." That logic may be all right for Indians, but it is no good for killing giants. Little problems can become giants with very few feedings, and we must either get rid of our Goliaths, or they will get rid of us.

The Magic Pitcher

Many years ago I heard a story that has remained with me in a very helpful kind of way ever since. It had to do with a kindly, generous man who owned a magic pitcher. When the neighborhood children playing in their small Alpine village became tired and thirsty they would enter this man's shop, where he would pour out ice-cold milk for their refreshment and pleasure. I was greatly impressed by this idea of an unending supply, which ensured that no matter how much was poured out, the pitcher never ran dry.

Most of the people of our world have always been haunted by scarcity. In many areas there are not enough of the good things to go around. To the many millions in want, the idea of a magic pitcher with an inexhaustible abundance has a wonderful appeal.

In more recent years, I have thought that maybe this idea was not as unusual as I had at first imagined. For example, most of our benefits come from *people* rather than from things, and we know many people who have some of the characteristics of the magic pitcher. I often think back to my mother and the unending supply of love, understanding, and help that she continually poured out upon ten children; and while I am aware of the contention of the scientists that there is no such thing as perpetual motion, yet my mother didn't miss it by very much.

Besides my mother, I think of my Heavenly Father as having a kind of magic pitcher from which he is continually pouring for our benefit if we merely hold up our glasses. Through Malachi he said, "Prove me now herewith . . . if I will not open you the windows of heaven, and pour you out a blessing, that there shall not be room enough to receive it" (Malachi 3:10). And yet his own supply does not become less. He said through Isaiah, "I will pour my spirit upon thy seed, and my blessing upon thine offspring" (Isaiah 44:3). Peter quoted the word of the Lord, saying, "And it shall come to pass in the last days, saith God, I will pour out of my Spirit upon all flesh: and your sons and your daughters shall prophesy, and your young men shall see visions, and your old men shall dream dreams" (Acts 2:17).

In many ways we resemble the story children at their play who depend for their welfare upon others. Of course, the greatest need that any of us have is for God. God created us. He gives us life. Every day he is sending us energy, food, and vitality from the sun. The Psalmist expressed a part of our need when he said, "My soul thirsteth for God" (Psalm 42:2). As our souls thirst, or as we tire in our play, or as we need direction and counsel, we may go to our Heavenly Father and receive refreshment and inspiration according to our need.

In her poem "The Gate of the Year," M. Louise Haskins gives a key to our receiving this direction:

> And I said to the man who stood at the gate of the year:
> "Give me a light, that I may tread safely into the unknown."
> And he replied:
>
> "Go out into the darkness and put
>   your hand into the hand of God.
> That shall be to you better than
>   light and safer than a known way."

God gives us many things. But probably one of the most important is that he has given us a kind of magic pitcher of our own, and the second greatest commandment has to do with filling the glasses of our fellowmen. We understand a great deal about our right to receive inspiration and blessings from God, and what a thrilling thought it is that we may entitle ourselves to a flow of inspiration from the very source of all intelligence and power! But there is another wonderful privilege that we do not always understand, and that is our right to *give* inspiration to others.

We are the children of God and have been endowed with our Father's potentialities. We are not like mere cisterns capable only of receiving the living waters; we may also open some springs in our own lives. We hope to someday become even as God, and one of the chief characteristics of godliness is giving out. This is an ability that *we already have.* From our magic pitchers we may pour out many benefits to enrich and sweeten other lives. Enos wrote, "I did pour out my whole soul unto God for [my brethren] (Enos 1:9). And we may also pour out our souls for the benefit of our brothers and sisters. Of course, what we pour out depends upon what our pitchers contain.

I remember a great teacher of my youth who filled my cup from her store of spirituality and faith. For almost everything I am indebted to someone, and I hope to be able to discharge my debt in relieving some of the scarcity by pouring out encouragement or determination into someone else's cup. I pray that God will accept my humble offerings to his other children as the only method of repayment within my reach for his bounties to me. One of the greatest gifts anyone can make to his fellowmen is a sincere good example, for more than almost any other thing we need to see before us a real live working model of righteousness. What is more inspiring than to see real faith and godliness in actual operation? And one of the most exciting things about such a situation is that the more one pours from his magic pitcher, the more he has left.

In spite of the scientific marvels and undreamed-of wonders of our day, nothing has yet been discovered that approaches the wonder of a great human being, with his special talents to help others. Some people inspire others through the power of their music. Others change lives by an outpouring of stimulating thoughts. The magic pitchers of some are filled with the inspiration of the great literature of the world. The canvasses of a great painter are given the power to inspire people.

Whatever his gift, each child of God was intended to be an

artist in his own right and in his own way. Some have their magic pitchers filled with the sacred scriptures and pour out the word of the Lord and make it memorable in other lives. There are some people who, like the actor Charles Laughton, can get people to pay money to hear the scriptures read. Mr. Laughton didn't read anything to them that they couldn't read for themselves. The very ideas they paid money to hear they had already heard many times before. But they liked to hear Mr. Laughton rerun these ideas as he poured out his heart with them. It is reported that a group of people actually paid $3.50 each to hear Mr. Laughton read a laundry list.

People can increase the effectiveness of ideas. Every human being has a kind of radioactivity of spirit which adds power and importance to words. When great ideas are supercharged with enthusiasm and underlined with conviction, and when the soul is poured out with them, they have a greater power to lift people up.

One day while walking down the street, I met a good friend whom I had not seen for some time. After a friendly visit I continued on my way, but I felt that something had been added to me by the contact. I was stronger and better than before, and I pondered on the pleasant and profitable experience it can be to be charged with the radiations that can come from a great human being. Then I thought that if I knew all there was to know about the *other* people I was passing on the street, it would be quite likely that every one of them had the power to inspire me, and I might do the same for them.

Inspired books are available to us. We have inspiring experiences. But the greatest of all good is an inspiring person. We are kept fairly conscious of the influence that others may have in *our* lives, but we lose track of the benefits that we ourselves may pour out. We are aware of how pleasant it is to be on the receiving end of inspiration, and in that context we may feel like the Psalmist, who said, "My cup runneth over" (Psalm 23:5). But our highest rank is attained when we take our position on the giving end of inspiration. As Paul told the elders from Ephesus, "It is *more blessed* to *give* than to receive" (Acts 20:35, emphasis added).

We need to increase the awareness of our ability as givers. Some people stay away from their church meetings because they feel they don't receive anything. But those who go to church to give something are the ones whose cups are usually running over.

It has always been interesting to me to hear people talk about their missionary experiences. The thing that frequently impresses us about our missions are the pleasant things that happen to us. But the greatest role of a missionary is for *him* to happen to other people. The Lord said, "Ye are not sent forth to be taught, but to teach" (D&C 43:15). The Lord expects us to always have our magic pitchers ready, and *we* must be ready also, for before anyone can deliver a great message he must *be* a great messenger. There must be inspiration in the pitcher, but there must be genuineness and power in the one who pours it out.

We might well borrow a trait from Winston Churchill. It was said that he not only *studied* history, he made it. He was the *source* of great events. When England and the world were about to be overcome by the mechanized might of Nazi arms, Winston Churchill went on the radio and poured out his inexhaustible courage and "will to win" into the cups of his countrymen. He said:

> We shall not flag or fail. We shall go on to the end, we shall fight in France, we shall fight on the seas and oceans, we shall fight with growing confidence and growing strength in the air, we shall defend our island, whatever the cost may be, we shall fight on the beaches, we shall fight on the landing grounds, we shall fight in the fields and in the streets, we shall fight in the hills; we shall never surrender, and even if, which I do not for a moment believe, this island or a large part of it were subjugated and starving, then our Empire beyond the seas, armed and guarded by the British fleet, would carry on the struggle, until, in God's good time, the New World, with all its power and might, steps forth to the rescue and the liberation of the old.

Probably more than any other individual, Churchill was responsible for the victory of the free world.

We ourselves also have some victories to win. We can help righteousness to win over sin, faith over doubt, and knowledge over ignorance. And as we pour out, God increases the level of our own supply. Jesus said, "Give, and it shall be given unto you; good measure, pressed down, and shaken together, and running over" (Luke 6:38). He who gives, receives. He who keeps, loses. To make sure that our pitcher will never run dry, we should keep pouring. We pour out enthusiasm, conviction, love, godliness and the power of a good example, and lo, our own lives are soon overflowing.

Next in importance only to the revelation that comes from God is the inspiration that comes from God's greatest creation, man. We can give encouragement, stir up enthusiasm, develop faith, and add zest to life. Jesus said, "Man shall not live by bread alone" (Matthew 4:4). And as Jesus received his strength from doing the will of his Heavenly Father, so we grow in power, not by being only a receiving station, but also by being a generating plant. We may be partly storage batteries, but we are also dynamos. The most worthwhile human being is a combination of storage battery and dynamo, of reservoir and spring.

Four hundred years before Christ, Socrates went around in ancient Athens asking people questions, getting them to think straight and make decisions binding upon themselves. He not only filled their cups but also helped them to increase their own flow to others. On one occasion Socrates was sitting with some friends at dinner. In those days they sat in a circle on the floor partially leaning against each other. Socrates said that as water could be made to run by means of a siphon from a fuller to an emptier cask, so knowledge and faith ran from the greater to the lesser among men. As we increase our generating power we raise the level of our own supply. Then our flow to others is easier, as it is pretty difficult to get water to run uphill.

Jesus is our greatest example in giving. He said, "I am come that they might have life, and that they might have it more abundantly" (John 10:10). Drinking from his unending supply, tax collectors and fishermen became prophets and apostles. He also opened new sources of power in them and then sent them out to fill the glasses of others. The very foundation on which his church is built is revelation from God, and the process by which his work is carried on is for us to pour out to each other. We need inspiring work; we must have inspiring workers.

In the Twenty-third Psalm, David sang what is probably the greatest and most moving expression of the Lord's pouring-out process:

> The Lord is my shepherd; I shall not want.
>
> He maketh me to lie down in green pastures: he leadeth me beside the still waters.
>
> He restoreth my soul: he leadeth me in the paths of righteousness for his name's sake.
>
> Yea, though I walk through the valley of the shadow of death, I will fear no evil: for thou art with me; thy rod and thy staff they comfort me.
>
> Thou preparest a table before me in the presence of mine enemies; thou anointest my head with oil; my cup runneth over.
>
> Surely goodness and mercy shall follow me all the days of my life: and I will dwell in the house of the Lord forever.

As our own cups overflow with the blessings from our Heavenly Father, may we pour out a full measure to his other children.

The Old Rugged Cross

The Reverend George Bennard was a deeply religious young man who lived when our twentieth century was just getting under way. As an officer in the Salvation Army and later as an interdenominational evangelist, he participated in many religious meetings in Michigan and New York. As he went about trying to build up faith and spirituality in people, he felt a strong desire to write a poem worthy of the religion of Christ, one that would fill an emotional need in people's lives.

In an extraordinary way, George Bennard felt the spirit of that great scriptural passage that says, "For God so loved the world, that he gave his only begotten Son, that whosoever believeth in him should not perish, but have everlasting life" (John 3:16). It was George Bennard's thought that these lines reminding us of the Redeemer's sacrifice serve to sum up almost the entire enterprise of human salvation. It seemed to him that the cross on which Christ died might serve better than anything else as an emblem of God's relationship with men.

Later on, in 1912, while working in Albion, Michigan, George Bennard did write his poem, and it was centered in the cross on which Christ completed his sacrifice. Appropriately enough, he entitled his poem, "The Old Rugged Cross." After it was set to music, it soon won popular acclaim and was sung everywhere. Since that time, many people have had great joy in the symbolism that Reverend Bennard pictured, and they have also been delighted by the beauty and comfort they have received as they have run this sentiment through their minds and hearts.

Since this hymn was written, there have been many times when in trouble or while in worship that people have received a great spiritual uplift by singing the familiar refrain.

> On a hill far away stood an old rugged cross,
> The emblem of suff'ring and shame;
> And I love that old cross where the dearest and best
> For a world of lost sinners was slain.

> Chorus
>
> So I'll cherish the old rugged cross,
> Till my trophies at last I lay down;
> I will cling to the old rugged cross,
> And exchange it some day for a crown.

> Oh, that old rugged cross, so despised by the world,
> Has a wondrous attraction for me;
> For the dear Lamb of God left His glory above,
> To bear it to dark Calvary.

> In the old rugged cross, stain'd with blood so divine,
> A wondrous beauty I see;
> For 'twas on that old cross Jesus suffered and died,
> To pardon and sanctify me.

> To the old rugged cross I will ever be true,
> Its shame and reproach gladly bear;
> Then He'll call me some day to my home far away,
> Where His glory forever I'll share.

It is a very interesting fact that even before the Master's death, the term *cross* was often used by him as a symbol for man's loyalty to God. The burden of carrying the cross was intended then, as now, as a test of the devotion and righteousness of those who counted themselves followers of the Son of God. Jesus said to his disciples: "If any man will come after me, let him deny himself, and take up his cross, and follow me" (Matthew 16:24).

By this picturesque statement, the Lord meant to convey a much greater meaning than that his followers should merely acknowledge the name of Christ. The burden of the cross is represented by the more difficult and more enduring *works* that give our faith its life. Contrary to what some believe, Christianity is not just something to acknowledge or to think about, it is something to do and to be. To take up the cross of Christ and to follow him means not only to be informed about his program but also to learn to do the things that he has asked us to do. There are many people who honor God with their lips and pay him tribute when things are going well. He himself pointed out one of our human weaknesses when he said: "They draw near to me with their lips, but their hearts are far from me, they teach for doctrines the commandments of men, having a form of godliness, but they deny the power thereof" (Joseph Smith—History:19). Of course, we pass one of our best religious tests when we are willing to demonstrate our faith by taking up the cross of Christ and actually doing the job assigned to us.

There were many who followed Jesus merely hoping to receive some benefit from his miracles. And as in days of old, so there are many now who would far rather eat of his loaves and fishes than carry his cross. Before that eventful crucifixion some nineteen hundred years ago, Jesus stumbled blindly toward Calvary. He needed the assistance of a strong, vigorous person to help him carry the load of the literal cross. Because no one volunteered, this duty was forced upon one Simon, the Cyrenian (Matthew 27:32). That this service to the Master was a thrilling opportunity Simon perhaps did not realize at the moment, yet this small amount of forced labor is the one thing for which Simon is remembered. This privilege of carrying the cross of Christ is likewise our greatest opportunity. Our greatest chance to be remembered will be because we have done some good in his name. This greatest of all calls is now before us. Jesus is still saying to us, "take up your cross, follow me" (D&C 112:14). We should follow him in his faith and in his righteousness and in his willingness to serve.

In speaking to his followers, the Master used another interesting figure of speech when he said, "Take my yoke upon you" (Matthew 11:29). Apparently Jesus had spent a good deal of time in the carpenter shop, and he probably had made many yokes to fit the necks of oxen. The yoke was a device to enable them to increase the amount of work they were capable of doing without hurting their necks. To carry the cross seems like a little more serious kind of work than merely to wear a yoke. One who uses the yoke effectively may be a good worker, but to carry the cross is the job of a believer, a disciple, and a friend.

Jesus spoke a great line that also applies to all of us in our day when he said, "He that taketh not his cross, and followeth after me, is not worthy of me" (Matthew 10:38). Those who carry the cross are the real identifiers with Christ. They *believe,* but even more important, they are willing to *do* the work involved. They are also willing to suffer a little bit if that is necessary, and in all other ways they desire to help the Savior of men in his efforts to bring about the eternal salvation of human beings. It doesn't help very much merely to support him with our words or even with our testimonies if, during the critical moments, we withdraw our strength and let him carry the cross alone.

Therefore, if we would like to put our Christian patience, virtue, and actual good works to the test, we might measure our ability and our endurance in carrying the cross of Christ. This represents our greatest opportunity in a world that is filled with great opportunities. There is an urgent need among us for someone to help establish the doctrines of Christ in the minds of people. The real Christians are the men and women who are willing to fight for the right when necessary, instead of being carried along by the evil of the world. Simon from Cyrene carried the cross of Christ up to the top of Calvary. Like Simon, we are also strong and possess great power and influence. Just think what could be accomplished if, with one accord, all would set their hearts on doing the Lord's work. Even one man can, if he will, change the morale of the whole community.

The cross has a kind of universal acceptance as the symbol of Christianity. But it might also represent the two most important commandments. In its physical makeup, the cross has vertical as well as horizontal dimensions. These are the same two dimensions possessed by the gospel of Christ. In both the gospel and the cross, the vertical standards point from the earth upward toward God. Certainly this upright standard fittingly represents the first of the two greatest commandments as it constantly reminds us to do our duty to our Heavenly Father.

To complete the picture, the horizontal bar reaches out toward our fellowmen in love and service and therefore fittingly represents the second of the two great commandments. King Benjamin said that when we are in the service of our fellowmen we are in the service of God (Mosiah 2:17). And in the religion of the Master, next only to the follower's love of the Father is his love of his fellowmen and his desire to be of service to them. What a thrilling thing it would be for us to wholeheartedly identify our lives with these two great objectives symbolically represented by the old rugged cross!

In his poem, George Bennard indicates how one might feel if he had a strong emotional attachment to this symbol and the things for which it stands. Actually many things are not important for themselves alone. Frequently they are even more important for what they stand for in our minds and what they get us to do. We have many great symbols by which we live, among which are a ring on the finger, a light in the window, and a flag in the breeze. But the old rugged cross comes in a little different category. It might appropriately represent the most tremendous facts in the universe: that the Son of God gave his life for us, and it is by his stripes that we are healed.

The vertical standard of the cross makes us conscious of that great commandment that says, "Thou shalt love the Lord thy God with all thy heart, and with all thy soul, and with all thy mind, and with all thy strength" (Mark 12:30). By obedience to this commandment, we could entitle ourselves to receive all the blessings of God. We could get an unlimited amount of inspiration and direction direct from the source of all intelligence and power. If we really love him and serve him, we will become like him. But this commandment is only a part of the thesis of the gospel. The second part of our religion is one of love and activity that reaches out in its horizontal dimension of service to our fellowmen.

We must do something about this opportunity while it is still available. In *Julius Caesar,* Shakespeare has Brutus say:

> There is a tide in the affairs of men,
> Which, taken at the flood, leads on to fortune;
> Omitted, all the voyage of their life
> Is bound in shallows and in miseries.
> On such a full sea are we now afloat;
> And we must take the current when it serves,
> Or lose our ventures.

But in spite of all of the warnings, so many of our Christian enterprises are lost because of lethargy and procrastination in us. Members of one organizaton were shocked when their secretary read to them a list of forty-six resolutions they had passed during a certain year, resolutions on which no action had ever been taken. As followers of Christ, most of us also have a lot of unfulfilled resolutions. Nothing is ever settled merely by passing resolutions, however excellent they may be. Certainly we must constantly beware of the great sins of fractional devotion and minimum performance and marginal morals.

Soldiers sometimes refer to a situation called "fox-hole religion." There are some people who turn to God only in the pinches of desperation or when something is troubling them. However, the most unhealthy kind of a God-seeker is like the man who neglects his friends until he needs a loan.

Our greatest opportunity always will be found in the formula given by Jesus: Deny yourself; take up the cross; follow him. This is the way we establish in our lives those important traits that are recommended by the symbolism of the old rugged cross. May God help us to carry it nobly.

The Chambered Nautilus

One of the distinguishing characteristics of great men and women is that they usually have a larger than average number of sources from which they can learn. People have trouble when they don't progress effectively, and no matter how favorable the environment may be, learning presents a difficult problem for some people. Even in a great university where conditions are made as favorable as can be, many students have problems. Some fight learning by cutting classes. They put off study and resist any enthusiasm to work at their own education. Some have only half made up their minds to learn, and some allow distractions to seriously upset their progress.

Only a comparatively small percentage of those who begin college are still there to finish the course. And even many of those who stick it out get only a small fraction of the possible benefit. And so it is in life. We miss many of our opportunities almost completely, and drag our feet on many others. Very early in our careers we reach a learning plateau from which we never progress substantially. Many of us are no farther ahead at sixty than we were at fifty. Frequently we don't have any better attitudes at forty than we had at thirty. Our faith may be no greater at seventy than at sixty, and we are often farther away from God at eighty than we were at seventy.

It is a sad fact that some people make very little progress during their entire lifetime, yet others learn from everything and everyone around them. James Watt invented the steam engine after watching a boiling teakettle. Eli Whitney invented the cotton gin after seeing a cat try to pull a chicken backwards through a picket fence. Robert Bruce built up enough determination to win freedom for the Scots while watching a spider persist after repeated failures until it reached its goal.

Shakespeare pointed out some of these effective learners as those who found tongues in trees, books in running brooks, sermons in stones, and good in everything. Jesus himself was the greatest master of this art of observation that leads to learning. As far as we are aware, Jesus had no extended formal schooling. In his lifetime he probably never traveled any great distance from his home, yet from the most simple experiences he learned some of the greatest lessons which present-day wise men are still studying.

In his parable of the sower, Jesus gave us some of the thoughts that went through his mind as he watched the farmer sowing his wheat. He also taught great lessons out of the experiences of the prodigal son, the good Samaritan, the wise and foolish virgins, the tax money, the tribute money, the talents, and the pearl of great price. Whether an event was good or bad in itself, Jesus made a lesson of good from it. He even drew strength from his own temptations, and every other experience he ever had was made to promote some useful purpose. Even Satan himself is permitted in this world to serve our best interests. For as we resist evil and struggle against weakness, we develop our characters and become stronger and more determined. Every failure should recharge our determination to rise *above* failure, and every success should build up our enthusiasm to increase the volume of our total accomplishment.

The Apostle Paul said, "All things work together for good to them that love God" (Romans 8:28). What a great idea! That is, if we love God, if we think right, if we have the right attitude, then everything works for our benefit and we learn from everybody and everything.

In 1858 Oliver Wendell Holmes published a stimulating poem entitled "The Chambered Nautilus." It is the story of the life and development of a little shelled animal called the pearly nautilus, which spends its life in a series of successively enlarging physical compartments. As the nautilus grows, it builds an ever-widening spiral shell which is divided into chambers by transverse curved partitions of shelly matter. As it increases in size, its former habitation becomes inadequate, and therefore it moves into the larger and more suitable house, for which it has foreseen the need and provided the accommodation. As each change is made, it occupies only the last and outermost compartment.

On one occasion, a little girl visited Dr. Holmes. His study contained many of the beautiful sea shells that had previously served as homes for these little animals. In order to more clearly explain his poem to his young visitor, Dr. Holmes took one of these shells and sawed it in two crosswise. Then he could clearly display to her the vacated sections to illustrate the animal's expanding way of life.

Because we are all interested in life's profound meanings, Dr. Holmes's poem serves us as a kind of symbol or pattern for our own lives. In its first stanza the author relates some of the traditional fancies that the poets have built up around the nautilus. In their poetic imaginations, this little craft is a ship of pearl which sails through enchanted seas where beautiful fabled sirens sing songs of unheard-of sweetness. And in the imagination it might be an echo of these siren songs that can be heard when a person puts an ocean shell up to his ear.

The second verse pictures the discarded lifeless shell. The occupant has now gone, and its dwellingplace has been sawn asunder so that onlookers may more clearly understand the marvelous growth program with which God has endowed this humble creature of his creation.

The third verse is a flashback to the life of the nautilus, and suggests the excellence of the toil that took place during its growing period. This after-view of the chambered nautilus's success may serve us as a preview of the possibilities of our own lives.

The fourth stanza is a rhapsody of thanksgiving for a heavenly message of progress and success. This stanza also serves as a prelude to the fifth stanza, which might well become the prayer of every aspiring human soul. Every child of God has been endowed with his own divine right for fulfillment through a thrilling series of growth experiences. "The Chambered Nautilus" is a beautiful poem and has a delightful philosophy, a message of appreciation, and an uplifting, eternal challenge. Our own lives take on meaning as we are able to translate the music, aspiration, and spirit of accomplishment into our own hearts.

When John Greenleaf Whittier first read this exquisite poem he pronounced his own verdict of its worth by saying that it was "booked for immortality." And Dr. Holmes himself prized this poem as one of the best he had ever written.

The Chambered Nautilus

This is the ship of pearl, which, poets feign,
 Sails the unshadowed main, —
 The venturous bark that flings
On the sweet summer wind its purpled wings
In gulfs enchanted, where the Siren sings,
 And coral reefs lie bare,
Where the cold sea-maids rise to sun their streaming hair.

Its webs of living gauze no more unfurl;
 Wrecked is the ship of pearl!
 And every chambered cell,
Where its dim, dreaming life was wont to dwell,
As the frail tenant shaped his growing shell,
 Before thee lies revealed, —
Its irised ceiling rent, its sunless crypt unsealed!

Year after year beheld the silent toil
 That spread his lustrous coil;
 Still, as the spiral grew,
He left the past year's dwelling for the new,
Stole with soft step its shining archway through,
 Built up its idle door,
Stretched in his last-found home, and knew the old no more.

Thanks for the heavenly message brought by thee,
 Child of the wandering sea,
 Cast from her lap, forlorn!
From thy dead lips a clearer note is born
Than ever Triton blew from wreathèd horn!

While on mine ear it rings,
Through the deep caves of thought I hear a voice that sings:—

Build thee more stately mansions, O my soul,
    As the swift seasons roll!
    Leave thy low-vaulted past!
Let each new temple, nobler than the last,
Shut thee from heaven with a dome more vast,
    Till thou at length art free;
Leaving thine outgrown shell by life's unresting sea!

I thought of a contrast to the chambered nautilus the other day as a discouraged salesman was telling about some of his problems. For the first three years his occupational record had shown that, like the nautilus, he had also made steady improvement, so that each period found him substantially ahead of where he had previously been. Then he began allowing some distracting occupational sins to take his mind from what he was doing, and consequently his shell stopped expanding and began to shrink. If he had been a pearly nautilus, he would have had a pretty tight squeeze trying to live in a financial house that was only half the size of the one he had occupied during the previous year. These distractions had also done a considerable amount of damage by shrinking up the personality house in which he had lived. The discouragement and lethargy caused by his distractions had started a backward movement, making him smaller and weaker than he had formerly been. As this belittling process continued, he lost a considerable amount of his faith and self-confidence.

For the next few months he made a forced effort in trying for a comeback, but he had lost the spirit of growth, and the beautiful songs of success no longer echoed in his heart. When one has a broken spirit, a comeback is sometimes pretty difficult. God can resurrect a dead body, but who can resurrect a dead faith, or powerize a sick attitude, or cleanse a sinful heart? Many alcoholics, criminals, and other sinners have frequently so belittled themselves that they have found it difficult to get back the growth spirit of the chambered nautilus.

Success is always so much more simple when one makes steady year-by-year progress in building up his faith and getting greater power into his self-confidence. For after one lives in a rut for a long enough time, or cultivates too many reverse attitudes, he loses the spirit of that song of success that is often pretty hard to recover. We don't take much joy in any accomplishment that doesn't have an expanding pattern. There can be a lot of fun in working one's way from a hovel to a mansion, but there is no joy in having to hide one's pride and move out of the mansion to again occupy the hovel. Life has been given to us as the greatest gift that even God can provide. And our days represent that precious time allotted to us in which to go forward. It is a serious misuse of life when we spend our inheritance floundering around or thrashing up and down without progress or direction. We should never permit any situation where a clear view of our lives would disclose that a worsening process was making our living compartments smaller and less desirable.

In speaking of one of those who followed the opposite course of deterioration, the scripture says, "It had been good for that man if he had not been born (Matthew 26:24). We need a particular control over both our life's compass and its speedometer. Sometimes we grow very rapidly in certain periods, and then we allow adverse influences or a series of demerits to send us back toward zero.

Homer, the ancient author of the *Odyssey*, tells the story of Ulysses and his men visiting the magic isles while returning from the battle of Troy. As a punishment to some of these men for what they had done, the story says, they were turned into swine. But we often perform a similar feat by turning our lives into something less than they were and thereby we bring upon ourselves a punishment that is most unpleasant.

In the financial and occupational departments of our lives our progress is often promoted by the urging of necessity. But in the mental and spiritual fields we frequently do not have the same pressure from behind and we therefore frequently pick up some bad habits that turn our course downward. At one time King Saul was the goodliest person in Israel, but his disobedience to God and the evil spirit that it engendered brought on a serious retrogression, and he died a suicide. Solomon was once the wisest man who ever lived. He saw the Lord twice, but when he began violating the laws on which his wisdom had been granted, the blessings were withdrawn, and he too began that long, hard journey downhill. He provided an idolatrous mother for his son Rehoboam who would follow him upon the throne. He led his own people into idolatry and slavery, and he himself died a partial idolator, very much out of favor with God.

Lucifer, who was once a son of the morning, ended up as Satan, and Judas the apostle of Jesus Christ became his Master's betrayer and finally hanged himself. There is no benefit or happiness in walking down that broad road toward making our lives into zeros.

Most of our ultimate success will depend on how well we have lived the philosophy of the chambered nautilus. If each year we can fill a little bigger compartment than we did the year before, we will always be looking in the right direction. This involves the processes of eliminating evil and filling our lives with faith and the kind of righteousness, industry, devotion, obedience, and service that will help us to reach our destiny in becoming like God. Therefore we again offer up our own life's prayer as we sing:

> Build thee more stately mansions, O my soul,
>> As the swift seasons roll!
>> Leave thy low-vaulted past!
> Let each new temple, nobler than the last,
> Shut thee from heaven with a dome more vast,
>> Till thou at length art free;
> Leaving thine outgrown shell by life's unresting sea!

The Thinker

From time to time we come across a representation of an interesting little statue called *The Thinker*. It shows a man in a sitting position with his elbow on his knee and his chin resting on his hand. His attitude and expression indicate that he is absorbed in deep meditation. This little image is usually displayed in homes or offices as an ornament. But its more subtle purpose is to remind us of that interesting mental process wherein various kinds of good ideas, programs, and images are formed in the mind to bring about some useful accomplishment. The original of this statue was carved by the French sculptor Auguste Rodin, who died in 1917. He was a noted realist, and some of his other sculptured creations were *The Hand of God, The Prayer*, and *Adam and Eve*. Mr. Rodin became famous for his visual portrayal of great ideas.

It has been said that the importance of a thing is not always found in the object itself; that it may have an even greater value for what it stands for, or is a sign of, or serves as a symbol for. And what greater idea could anyone cultivate than the one symbolized by Mr. Rodin's image? We have one of our greatest human experiences when we get an active idea working in our minds. There is nothing more exciting or worthwhile than that which a good mind can do with an idea.

Someone has stimulated us with the question, "How would you like to create your own mind?" but isn't that exactly what we all do? William James said, "The mind is made up by what it feeds upon." The mind, like the dyer's hand, is colored by what it holds. If I hold in my hand a sponge full of purple dye, my hand becomes purple, and if I hold in my mind and heart the great ideas of faith, love, ambition, and devotion to God, my whole personality is colored accordingly. Even our souls themselves are fashioned by what and how we think. The finest creation of God is a great human being, and the mind was created to be its presiding officer.

However, this great resource has some reverse possibilities. When we think negative thoughts we develop negative minds. Some people have morose minds. Some have created depraved minds that produce a poisonous fruit in the form of depraved, degrading thoughts. The scriptures point out that some people will be damned. And we might try to imagine what it would be like to have a damned mind and forever feed on the evil, darkness, and depression of damned thoughts.

On the other hand, think of this godly privilege: We may now engage in that tremendous process of developing celestial minds that will think only celestial, constructive, happy thoughts. These are the kinds of thoughts that God thinks. We should get as much mileage as possible from the fact that our future success will be determined by what we presently think. Physically we become what we eat, but mentally, spiritually, socially, and morally we become what we think. And we may think as big and as straight and as high as we like.

Napoleon Hill wrote a great book, *Think and Grow Rich.* We can also think and grow wise. We can think and grow faithful, and we can think and grow godly. Nor does being a great thinker require us to think only original thoughts. All of the greatest thoughts about love, beauty, faith, kindness, and success have already been thought again and again. But as we rerun them through our own minds they produce an increasing rate of return.

At birth almost everything, including ideas, is small and poorly formed. But thoughts can grow and become more perfect as they are rethought, and with the tremendous expansion of our literature we now have a far wider selection of ideas from which to choose than we have ever had before. We may select for our own rethinking those ideas that are in their most developed form.

If we run through our minds the same kind of thoughts that ran through the minds of Shakespeare, Emerson, Lincoln, or the Apostle Paul, our minds will eventually come to respond as did the minds of Shakespeare, Emerson, Lincoln, and the Apostle Paul. According to its use the mind develops a set of markings about as characteristic as our fingerprints. And when a great idea is run through our minds enough times, it may make an even greater improvement in us than it did in the man who thought it originally.

Thinking a great thought originally may not be nearly as important as applying one that has already been thought by someone else. Sometimes it takes a long time to think a thought through from birth to maturity. But we may take the greatest ideas that are now fully developed and available in their finest form, and use them to the limit of our ability in developing the most favorable characteristics in our own minds. We might even improve on Mr. Rodin's idea and dedicate a statue to the *re*thinker. It is only natural that the rethinker can show the greatest profit because of his larger volume and his greater selection.

Over a century ago my great-grandmother walked across the plains to help make a home for me in the valleys of the Rocky Mountains. Her labor helped to redeem a wilderness and make a forbidding desert to "blossom as the rose." As a grown man, I moved into the city that she and thousands of others had built. The temple had been completed. The streets had been paved, the light lines were up, the sewers were in, and many other conveniences had been built and paid for. And for my entire lifetime I have had far more benefits from their enterprise than they did who built them. They toiled to produce what they never lived to enjoy.

We have the same situation in regard to our ideas. We have had the great scriptures handed down to us free of charge, which cost the lives of many of the prophets and apostles who wrote them. As Christians we not only have what the ancients had, but we have the judgment of time shining upon the life of Christ and the voices of many additional witnesses bearing testimony of his divinity. Without effort on our part we have more of the word of the Lord than all previous generations combined. The scriptures also tell of the successes and failures of the lives they wrote about in a way that the writers themselves did not fully understand. We may have the profit that their lives produced without taking their risks or making their mistakes.

Jesus rethought the same ideas many times and then said, "Follow me." What a thrilling challenge that each of us can follow him in his thinking and can develop the courage and good works that make future good thoughts possible! The more we rethink the thoughts of Deity, the deeper our mental grooves become, the broader are the marks left on our character, and the more readily we are able to mold ourselves into the image of his righteousness. How tragic when we comprehend some great Christian ideal and then say, "I never gave it another thought"! If we rethink the Master's thoughts enough times and with enough intensity, our lives will tend to respond as his did.

There are many interesting word combinations denoting our mental activities. We speak of "thinking," or of "thinking it through," or of "thinking it over." With our thoughts we make plans, organize philosophies, and direct the most important of all values, which is our own lives. and when we put on our thinking caps and keep them on and keep them working, we may cause the most constructive elements in our lives to take on their most attractive appearance. Any mind becomes more productive as it develops the thinking attitudes, the ability to conceive, the power to visualize, and the ambition to build images, have dreams, and project the soul forward and upward.

John Milton said, "The mind in its own place, and of itself can make a heaven of hell or a hell of heaven." The mind can also do almost any other thing that it sets up for itself. Of course, this wonderful mental ability must be powerized and given direction. Someone has said that there is nothing more dangerous than an animated blind horse. Improperly directed thoughts can quickly mold us into something that we don't want to be.

During the long conflict between ancient Rome and Carthage, Cato, the old Roman Senator, ended every speech by saying, "Carthage must be destroyed." This technique for stamping an important idea into people's minds by "rethinking" has a counterpart in Winston Churchill's "V" sign for victory, which he used to flash around on everyone during World War II.

A great sales corporation adopted another victory slogan, which said, "Think five." They thought they could sell five billion dollars' worth of merchandise in one year, and they needed to get the goal firmly fixed in everyone's mind and have everyone feel a proper share of the responsibility. This idea to "think five" was lodged in everyone's mind with an importance great enough to give it special power. It became a kind of intercompany greeting that was on everyone's lips. As a means of implementing and reinforcing the objective, each member was asked to devise five specific ways of his own for bringing the company objective about.

Webster defines the word *engram* as "a hypothetical change in neural tissue postulated in order to account for persistence of memory." Business and military organizations have accomplished many miracles by their own processes for broadening the engrams and deepening the mental pathways leading to some objective firmly fixed in the minds of those concerned. But every child of God has the greatest of all objectives in making the best and the most of his own life. This requires that we have the right kind of thoughts in the "think tank" that supplies our minds. Each of us needs to have good, deep engrams leading to the goal. In the days of ancient Israel, the Lord instituted among the people the custom of wearing phylacteries. The Lord knew that there were certain ideas that were indispensable to their contemplated success. So he had the people memorize these success ideas and write them down on pieces of parchment, enclose them in little leather tubes, and wear them around their necks, on their hands, and in other places on their person where they would always be in sight.

He told them: "And these words, which I command thee this day, shall be in thine heart: and thou shalt teach them diligently unto thy children, and shalt talk of them when thou sittest in thine house, and when thou walkest by the way, and when thou liest down, and when thou risest up. And thou shalt bind them for a sign upon thine hand, and they shall be as frontlets between thine eyes." Some of the Israelites also wore these phylacteries upon their fingers like rings. On one of these phylacteries was inscribed the words: "Thou shalt love the Lord thy God with all thine heart, and with all thy soul, and with all thy might." (Deuteronomy 6:6-8, 5.)

The Lord prescribed this process of consolidation and joint action so that they could concentrate all of the elements of personal power into one determined effort. This formula containing one of the most important secrets of success involves a joint action of the heart, the mind, the soul, and the might. We can serve God with our minds, by our study, our thoughts, our understanding, and an uplifting mental attitude. We serve God with our hearts and souls, by our devotion, adoration, worship, and obedience. We serve God with our might, by the exercise of a firm determination, an unobstructed will power, and a vigorous physical activity. This kind of coordination places the greatest accomplishments within our easy reach.

Suppose we adopted a strong philosophy of thinking, and suppose that we were going to "think five." What would our strongest thoughts be? Daniel Webster said, "The greatest thought that has ever entered my mind is the consciousness of my individual responsibility to God." Jesus said, "And this is life eternal, that they might know thee the only true God, and Jesus Christ, whom thou hast sent" (John 17:3). Just suppose that we could actually get these thoughts firmly established in our minds.

William James said, "The greatest discovery of my generation is that you can change your circumstances by changing your attitudes of mind." Everyone wants to change his circumstances, but only a few are willing to change themselves. Leonardo da Vinci showed himself a thinker when he said, "Thou, oh God, doth sell us all good things at the price of labor." And Jesus said, "All things are possible to him that believeth" (Mark 9:23).

With this kind of faith operating in our minds, our lives can be outstandingly successful. May God help us to rethink his thoughts effectively.

Damon and Pythias

We have often been reminded of the advantages of filing our minds with good ideas. As we read the world's great literature, we tend to absorb the best from the lives of others and use it for our own uplift. We ought to put on our magnifying glasses occasionally and then very earnestly read the great success stories of the world. Such a course would fill our minds with the spirit of real achievement.

The quality of our lives would also be greatly increased if we read more frequently the world's great stories of love and friendship. Who could fail to be thrilled by recalling the experiences that ripened the love between David and Jonathan? Their common bond of friendship and trust strikes one of the high notes of the scriptures. The Bible says, "the soul of Jonathan was knit with the soul of David, and Jonathan loved him as his own soul" (1 Samuel 18:1).

Many people have had their lives lifted above the ordinary by a recital of the Bible story of Ruth and Naomi. After Ruth's husband had died, her widowed mother-in-law tried to get her to return to her own people and begin life anew with them. But Ruth said to Naomi: "Intreat me not to leave thee, or to return from following after thee: for whither thou goest, I will go; and where thou lodgest, I will lodge: thy people shall be my people, and thy God my God: . . . the Lord do so to me, and more also, if ought but death part thee and me." (Ruth 1:16–17.)

We can find other great vicarious experiences to fill our various needs. One of the most worthwhile satisfactions that ever comes to any human being is the feeling of absolute confidence in the integrity and ability of someone he loves. To get this feeling vicariously is second only to the real experience.

There is a stimulating old Roman legend about two famous friends who lived in the ancient city of Syracuse in Sicily, about 400 B.C. Their names were Damon and Pythias. The tyrant King Dionysius, who ruled Syracuse at the time, unjustly condemned Damon to death because he had been falsely accused of plotting against the king. Damon begged for three days of time in which to put his affairs in order before his death. He also desired to attend the wedding of his sister, who lived at a considerable distance away.

The cynical old king had heard of the unusual friendship existing between Damon and Pythias, but he did not believe that such a love and loyalty could exist between two friends as that which was reported to be binding Damon and Pythias together. The king decided that this would be a good opportunity to test their feelings for each other, so he told Damon that he would grant the three-day stay of execution if Pythias would stand as his surety, and would agree to die in his place if Damon did not return.

Damon told Pythias what the king had said, and Pythias promptly presented himself to be bound in Damon's stead.

In attending to his affairs, Damon had to travel over some very rough country, but by the morning of the third day he had wound up his business and was returning to his doom when some unforeseen difficulties began blocking his way. A poem recounting some of these problems was written by William Peter entitled "True Friendship." He wrote:

> The heavens interposed by bringing up a great tempest.
> And Damon had a roaring river to cross.

The poem continues:

> And when the poor pilgrim arrived at the shore,
> Swollen to torrents the rills
> Rushed in foam from the hills.
> And crash went the bridge in the whirlpool's wild roar.

An impassable flood now blocked Damon's way, and his time was running short. He was unable to get aid, so in desperation he threw himself into the wild, roaring flood waters and swam with superhuman strength—not to save his own life, but to save his friend Pythias. Damon sank, then rose, then swam again. By the greatest efforts he struggled on until at length "the shore was won."

He had hardly escaped from the perils of the flood when

A band of fierce robbers encompassed his way,
"What would ye?" he cried, "my life I have nought;
Nay, my life is the king's." Then swift having caught
A club from the nearest, and swinging it round
With might more than man's, he laid three on the ground,
While the rest hurried off in dismay.

But dispersing the robbers didn't end his troubles. He also had a desert to cross.

As the noon's scorching flame
Shoots through his frame,
He turns, faint and way-worn, to Heaven on High
From the flood and the foe,
"Thou'st redeemed me, and oh!
Thus, by thirst overcome, must I effortless lie,
And leave him, the beloved of my bosom to die?"

Despite all the obstacles Damon didn't stop. He made his way against every kind of difficulty in his Herculean effort to save his friend Pythias. Overcoming flood, robbers, fatigue, heat, and thirst, he finally came within sight of Syracuse. On the outskirts he was met by his own servant, who advised him to flee and save himself because Pythias had already been executed, and the king was now seeking Damon to put him to death also. The servant said of Pythias:

"No; nothing can save his dear head from the tomb;
So think of preserving thine own.
Myself, I beheld him led forth to his doom;
Ere this, his brave spirit has flown!
With confident soul he stood, hour after hour,
Thy return never doubting to see;

No sneers of the tyrant that faith could o'erpower,
Or shake his assurance in thee!"

Then Damon replied to the servant:

"And is it too late? and can I not save
His dear life? Then, at least, let me share in his grave,
Yes, death shall unite us! no tyrant shall say,
That friend to his friend proved untrue; he may slay,—
May torture,—may mock at all mercy and ruth,
But ne'er shall he doubt of our friendship and truth."

Damon continued to go forward as fast as he could, only to
find that the servant's information had been inaccurate.

'Tis sunset: and Damon arrives at the gate,
Sees the scaffold, and multitudes gazing up from below;
Already the victim is bared for his fate,
Already the deathsman stands armed for the blow;
When hark! a wild voice which is echoed around,
Shouts, "Stay!—'tis I—it is Damon, for whom he was bound."

And now they sink in each other's embrace,
And are weeping for joy and despair,
Not a soul, among thousands, but melts at their case,
Which swift to the monarch they bear;
Even he, too, is moved—feels for once as he ought—
And commands, that they both to his throne shall be brought.

Then alternately gazing on each gallant youth,
With looks of awe, wonder, and shame:—
"Ye have conquered!" he cried, "Yes, I see now the truth—
That friendship is not a mere name.
Go;—you're free; but, while life's dearest blessings you prove
Let one prayer of your monarch be heard,
That—his past sins forgot—in this union of love
And of virtue—you make him the third."

When King Dionysius saw real trust and friendship in operation he wanted these qualities for himself and asked to be included
with Damon and Pythias as the third member of this alliance
devoted to true loyalty and friendship.

To experience love and confidence in someone is one of the
most priceless virtues in life. Using a little different name, Jesus put

these qualities under the title of the second great commandment. There are very few things in the world that are more pleasant than to believe in someone, or to be believed in by someone. What a thrilling experience to have a feeling of absolute confidence in the integrity and ability of one you love, and to believe that no matter what may happen he will prove faithful to every trust!

Of course, one of the important ingredients in this situation is to make ourselves worthy of that trust. Then we may know within ourselves that we can and will fully support with our actions the faith and good opinions of our friends. And what greater compliment could anyone pay us than to trust us? Or think of the pleasure we can give to others by merely making ourselves deserving of their wholehearted confidence. Carried to its ultimate, this delightful quality is very closely allied to worship. The first article of faith says, "We believe in God. . . ." That not only means that we believe God exists, it also means that we know the kind of being he is, that we were created in his image and endowed with his potentialities; but it also means that we believe in him, that we trust him, that we believe that he knows his business, and that our affairs are safe in his hands.

Job had this kind of belief in God. In the midst of his sorest trials and afflictions he said, "Though he slay me, yet will I trust in him" (Job 13:15). But to be complete, this Damon and Pythias kind of relationship must go in both directions. So let's look at the other side of the picture and see how God felt about Job. The record shows God saying to Satan: "Hast thou considered my servant Job, that there is none like him in the earth, a perfect and an upright man, one that feareth God, and escheweth evil? and still he holdest fast his integrity, although thou movedst me against him, to destroy him without cause." (Job 2:3.) How would you like to have God say that about you?

One-half of the greatest idea I know of in the world is to believe in God. The other half of that idea is to conduct our lives so that God will believe in us. This idea does not belong only to religion, it is the most important idea in business, in the professions, in government, or in our social relationships. Everything that is right and good makes us better citizens and more worth-while individuals. What quality could help us more before God or with our fellowmen than this ability to get ourselves believed in and trusted by others?

By contrast we might look at this trait on the negative side. What can be more unpleasant than to be continually disap-pointed by someone you want to believe in. You may even love him, but because he lacks in basic character you cannot trust him. Such a person may borrow money but must be forced to pay it back. If you try to help him he will misinterpret your action. Give him information and you will be misquoted. Give him your confidence and he will betray you. Depend on him and you will be double-crossed. Give him employment and he will let you down. On every occasion he meets you with excuses, alibis, untruths, worthless promises, laziness, irresponsibility, and a low grade of accomplishment. What a great prayer someone uttered when he said:

> Great God, I ask thee for no meaner pelf
> Than that I may not disappoint myself.

One of the most cherished blessings in life, or in business success, or in religious worship, is to have something solid for your faith to cling to. A climbing vine needs a noncrumbling brick wall to climb. Damon and Pythias were each a brick wall for the other. If you want to be a really great human being, be the kind of person that anyone can cling to without fear, climb up on with confidence, and trust and believe in with love.

We can help develop these qualities in ourselves by a closer association with such great stories as Damon and Pythias, David and Jonathan, Ruth and Naomi. But then at the very top of the list we have the most inspiring of all of the accounts of love and trust in the experience and association of God the Father and his Son Jesus Christ. On at least four occasions the Father has intro-duced the Son by saying, "This is my Beloved Son, in whom I am well pleased." What a great ambition, if, like Dionysius, we each determined to qualify as a third member of this alliance, fully devoted and loyal to these great beings!

For like Jesus, each of us also is a son or daughter of God and is entitled to give our Heavenly Father the same kind of pleasure in our association that he gets from his most prominent son. We cannot reach our maximum accomplishments if we cannot say, "We believe in God." But then, to make the picture complete, our lives must be such that God can say that he believes in us.

Joseph Smith

It has been said that a nation's greatness is usually written in the biographies of its great men. Some of the reasons why America is great are the people who settled here, the motives they possessed, the standards they have lived by, and the ambitions they have developed. America is great because of the ideals that have been handed down by her people. The world has no greater resource than that of a great man.

Thomas Carlyle said, "You cannot look upon a great man without gaining something from him." The ancient Romans used to capitalize on this idea by making statues of their greatest Romans and setting them up in their homes. Then as they looked at the statue, they thought about the qualities of the man it represented, and as they thought about him, they borrowed his virtues for their own lives.

We have done something very similar in America in setting aside the birthdays of our great men and holding their lives up before our minds for consideration and review.

Some time ago I reread one of Abraham Lincoln's anti-slavery debates. Lincoln's opponent had argued that they could not afford to free the Southern slaves because there were some four million of them and each had an average value to his owner of approximately a thousand dollars. He reasoned that if they freed the slaves, they would upset the economy of this little group of people, the slave owners, by some four billion dollars, which they could not afford. But in addition, he said, who would take care of the corn, cotton, and tobacco crops?

When Lincoln came to the platform he brushed all of these considerations aside as immaterial. He said: "There is only one question you need to answer in order to decide the question of slavery and that is this: Is slavery right or is it wrong? Is it right for some men to hold other men in bondage?

Suppose that in the future, whenever we have a difficult problem come up, we apply Lincoln's formula for solving it. All we need to do is to ask ourselves, what is right and what is wrong. We are all made richer when we think of the great virtues of Abraham Lincoln.

There is another great American whose life and work has had, and in increasing measure will have, a very important influence upon our thinking. He was a contemporary of Abraham Lincoln, being a little over three years old when Lincoln was born. His name was Joseph Smith. He was the great American prophet, and I would like to hold up for your consideration some thoughts about him.

Any man's greatness is judged by the work he does. If he isn't great in what he does, he isn't great. It has been suggested that a man's worth to the world should be judged by the answers to four basic questions. Those questions are:

1. Who gave him his assignment?
2. What was the size and importance of the job he did?
3. How well did he do his work?
4. What did he leave to posterity?

First, who gave Joseph Smith his assignment? That is, who is it that says he is great? Sometimes Republicans believe a man great while the Democrats disagree. Or a son may make an appraisal of his father's virtues that does not harmonize with the general opinion.

It is a little difficult to appraise the calling of one of the prophets, who have received their assignments from God. Many of the prophets received their divine calling at a very early age. Noah was ordained at ten (D&C 107:52). Samuel had a personal visit from the Lord in the temple at Shiloh when he was just a child, probably age twelve (1 Samuel 3:10, 21). David was anointed king of ancient Israel when he was just a shepherd boy, and waited many years before ascending to the throne (1 Samuel 16:12). Joseph was sent into Egypt on an errand for the Lord when he was seventeen (Genesis 37:2). Jesus taught the wise men in the temple at twelve (Luke 2:42). Jeremiah was called when a mere child, probably around thirteen (Jeremiah 1:6). Mormon, one of the great prophets of pre-Columbus America, was called at age ten (Mormon 1:2). Joseph Smith received a visit from the Father and the Son at age fourteen (Joseph Smith—History:7).

The Lord has an interesting advantage in the selection of a great man because he knew each one in the spirit world before this life began. In the first chapter of the book of Jeremiah we find out when God selected Jeremiah. The prophet said: "Then the word of the Lord came unto me, saying, before I formed thee in the belly I knew thee; and before thou camest forth out of the womb I sanctified thee, and I ordained thee a prophet unto the nations. Then said I, Ah, Lord God! behold, I cannot speak: for I am a child." (Jeremiah 1:4–6.)

In one of the greatest visions ever given in the world we find out something about how the Lord works. Abraham was shown his own premortal existence, and he recorded that experience in these words:

> Now the Lord had shown unto me, Abraham, the intelligences that were organized before the world was; and among all these there were many of the noble and great ones;
> And God saw these souls that they were good, and he stood in the midst of them, and he said: These I will make my rulers; for he stood among those that were spirits, and he saw that they were good; and he said unto me: Abraham, thou art one of them; thou wast chosen before thou wast born." (Abraham 3:22–23.)

We believe that our standing in eternity will be influenced by our faithfulness in this life. It is also logical that our lives here were influenced by our premortal existence. We know that Jesus was ordained before he was born (John 1:1–12). The Prophet Joseph Smith said: "Every man who has a calling to minister to the inhabitants of the world was ordained to that very purpose in the grand council in heaven before this world was" (B. H. Roberts, *A Comprehensive History of the Church,* 6:364).

Question number two: What was the size and importance of the job done by Joseph Smith? Of course, it is not always possible to judge a situation fully when we are so close to it. But what kind of man would one expect the Lord to select to open and lead the greatest and last of all the gospel dispensations, the dispensation of the fulness of times?

The great prophets of old looked enviously down to our age of wonders and enlightenment. This is the greatest of all ages. This is the day that is to prepare for the glorious second coming of Christ to the earth. Almost every other dispensation was wiped out by apostasy and, that even applies to the dispensation of Jesus. But our dispensation has been given the promise that the gospel shall never again be taken from the earth. One could scarcely conceive a more important assignment for a mortal being than to stand at the head of the last dispensation.

The third question is, How well did he do his work? The following appraisal of the work of the Prophet Joseph Smith was given by Josiah Quincy, noted writer and distinguished citizen of Boston. Mr. Quincy interviewed Joseph Smith at Nauvoo, Illinois, just before his martyrdom. Later he wrote a book entitled *Figures from the Past,* in which he asked the question, "What historical American of the nineteenth century has exerted the most powerful influence upon the destinies of his countrymen?" Mr. Quincy then proceeded to answer his own question:

> It is by no means impossible that the answer to that interrogatory may be thus written: Joseph Smith, the Mormon prophet. And that reply, absurd as it doubtless seems to most men now living, may be an obvious commonplace to their descendants. History deals in surprises and paradoxes quite as startling as this. The man who establishes a great religion in this age of free debate, and who was and is today accepted by hundreds of thousands as a direct emissary from the most high, is not to be disposed of merely by pelting his memory with unsavory epithets.

The Prophet's contemporaries made this appraisal of his life after his death:

> Joseph Smith, the Prophet and Seer of the Lord, has done more, save Jesus only, for the salvation of men in this world, than any other man that ever lived in it. In the short space of twenty years,

he has brought forth the Book of Mormon, which he translated by the gift and power of God, and has been the means of publishing it on two continents; has sent the fulness of the everlasting gospel, which it contained, to the four quarters of the earth; has brought forth the revelations and commandments which compose this book of Doctrine and Covenants, and many other wise documents and instructions for the benefit of the children of men; gathered many thousands of the Latter-day Saints, founded a great city [Nauvoo], and left a fame and name that cannot be slain. He lived great, and he died great in the eyes of God and his people; and like most of the Lord's anointed in ancient times, has sealed his mission and his works with his own blood (D&C 135:3.)

The fourth question is, "What did he leave to posterity? Moses left us a great heritage, including the Ten Commandments." Isaiah, Ezekiel, Jeremiah and other Old Testament prophets left the Old Testament chapters that bear their names. Matthew, Mark, Luke, Peter, James, John, Paul, and others left a series of wonderful letters and other writings that have been of great service and inspiration to the world.

But Joseph Smith has given to the world three great *volumes* of new scripture setting forth the simple principles of the gospel. He has restored to the world the sure knowledge of a personal God. The Christian world says we believe in God. Joseph Smith says, in substance, "I know there is a God, for I have seen him." Joseph Smith has written that everyone may read in it an account of this greatest vision of which the world has a record.

He received several visits from Moroni, the American prophet of pre-Columbus times who delivered the Book of Mormon to us.

Through Joseph Smith, the Aaronic and Melchizedek Priesthoods have been restored to earth respectively by John the Baptist and by Peter, James, and John, who held the keys of these priesthoods in their own dispensations. Joseph Smith reestablished under direct command from God the ancient custom of building temples wherein special ordinances for the living and the dead can be performed that are not acceptable to God in any other place.

On March 27, 1836, the first temple of this dispensation was dedicated at Kirtland, Ohio. A few days later, on April 3, 1836, Joseph Smith and Oliver Cowdery retired to the temple pulpit around which veils were dropped, and after silent and solemn prayer they received the following vision and personal manifestation of the Lord. The Prophet recorded:

The veil was taken from our minds, and the eyes of our understanding were opened.

We saw the Lord standing upon the breastwork of the pulpit, before us; and under his feet was a paved work of pure gold, in color like amber.

His eyes were as a flame of fire; the hair of his head was white like the pure snow; his countenance shone above the brightness of the sun; and his voice was as of the sound of the rushing of great waters. (D&C 110:1-3.)

After this vision closed, the heavens were again opened unto us; and Moses appeared before us, and committed unto us the keys of the gathering of Israel from the four parts of the earth, and the leading of the ten tribes from the land of the north.

After this, Elias appeared, and committed the dispensation of the gospel of Abraham, saying that in us and our seed all generations after us should be blessed.

After this vision had closed, another great and glorious vision burst upon us; for Elijah the prophet, who was taken to heaven without tasting death, stood before us, and said:

Behold, the time has fully come, which was spoken of by the mouth of Malachi—testifying that he [Elijah] should be sent, before the great and dreadful day of the Lord come—

To turn the hearts of the fathers to the children, and the children to the fathers, lest the whole earth be smitten with a curse—

Therefore, the keys of this dispensation are committed into your hands; and by this ye may know that the great and dreadful day of the Lord is near, even at the doors. (D&C 110:11-16.)

The fact that many people do not believe this message is only following the pattern of the past, even of the days of Jesus himself. Not only do many not believe, but many will not even listen, even though thousands of members of the Church bear testimony that this message is true. All are invited to investigate and gain a witness for themselves.

Joseph Smith died a martyr at age thirty-eight. "Greater love hath no man than this," said the Savior, "that a man lay down his life for his friends" (John 15:13).

Crossing the Rubicon

In the second half of the first century B.C., two outstanding Roman generals—Pompey the Great in Italy and Julius Caesar in Gaul—were vying with each other for political power. To protect and extend his interests, Caesar was considering marching on the capital to take matters into his own hands.

This momentous decision would immediately precipitate a civil war and divide the Roman world between Pompey and Caesar. Caesar knew what the consequences would be if he tried and failed. He knew that many lives would be lost in any event. Surely he must have hesitated before arriving at so great a decision, for he knew there could be no hesitation after the decision was made. Caesar carefully considered every angle. He explored every possible alternative. Then he made up his mind. He gave the order to march.

With his army, Caesar came to the Rubicon, a small river in northern Italy that served as the boundary line of his assigned territory. The Rubicon was called "the sacred and inviolable." It was the line across which no general was ever allowed to pass without special permission from the Senate. If Caesar crossed the Rubicon into Italy it would be with the idea of making the entire Roman dominions subject to his will.

One part of Caesar's power came because of his ability to analyze a situation; another part came because of his habit of always finishing what he started. He was now starting the biggest undertaking of his life, to strike down the very heart of the Roman world. Caesar said, "The die is cast." That expression marked the point where deliberation ended and action began. There would now be no turning back. He threw himself into the waters of the Rubicon at the head of his legions and thereby changed the whole history of his country.

Since this important event two thousand years ago, the phrase "crossing the Rubicon" has been used to indicate some decisive action of great importance, usually an irrevocable one. In one way the action of Caesar might become a sort of pattern for us. Our first step is to know what we are doing; then we should carefully weigh the arguments. Then we should make a decision and be willing to stake everything upon our judgment. Once the decision has been made, every contrary thought should be banished. No energy should then be wasted in doubts, fears, or reconsiderations, and nothing should be left undone which would help to bring about the projected accomplishment.

Whether Caesar was right or wrong is not the point of this discussion. The point is that every one of us also has a Rubicon to cross, and we should learn what we can about making decisions both on a personal and a group basis, and then learn how to carry them through to accomplishment.

The greatest sermon ever spoken consisted of just three words. Jesus said, "Come, follow me." And one of the most important decisions we ever have to make is, What are we going to do about it? Will we follow him? Can we develop the personal strength of purpose or the leadership to make an adequate accomplishment possible, and if so, how?

When a Roman soldier joined the legions of Caesar, he took a pledge to hold the life of Caesar dearer than all else. That was his Rubicon. What should be our attitude who enlist in the service of the Lord? Should our responsibility be of a lesser order? Should our minds be less firmly made up? Should our service be less devoted than those who paid their allegiance to Caesar?

A certain man said to Jesus, "Lord, I will follow thee whithersoever thou goest" (Luke 9:57). Jesus warned him to think about what was involved. That is an important part of making up our minds. What would this man do when the winds of opposition began to blow? Jesus cautioned him about the dangers of vacillation, for "he who hesitates is lost." Jesus said it this way: "No man, having put his hand to the plow, and looking back, is fit for the kingdom of God" (Luke 9:62). That is a pretty strong statement, and it concerns every member of the Church.

It has always been one of our most difficult problems to make accurate decisions which are solid enough to stand firm under the pressures of life. Too frequently we find reasons for wavering or side-stepping or turning back. Lot's wife crossed her Rubicon, but she was not quite as well prepared as Caesar was. Lot's wife hadn't quite made up her mind. Therefore she looked back and was turned into a pillar of salt (Genesis 19:26).

There are far too many of us who are afflicted with the trait of making partial decisions; then we are continually looking back over our shoulders. For example, ask ten people to tell you what their goal in life is and exactly what their plan is for accomplishment. Most people have no very definite answers to these important questions. We never quite get around to settling once and for all even the most important questions. How many of us actually make firm decisions about our objectives for eternity, supported by concrete methods for their attainment? If some of us get to the celestial kingdom, it will be by a kind of "accident" brought on by circumstances or the continual urging of friends to do our duty. Some have not permanently resolved the question of tithing, liquor, honesty, tobacco, church attendance, or other personal church performance. Their activity depends too much upon the circumstance of the moment. How many of us have really decided about our own church leadership—its quality, quantity, continuity and method? Think about the high turnover in office, the less-than-effective work being done, the large number of resignations each year, the many startings and stoppings. Think how much time people spend in indecision, reconsideration, vacillation, and retreat.

We often decide something one way when we are at the top of our condition and then abandon our plans when the tide begins to ebb. It is easy to get cold feet or weak knees when a challenging set of circumstances confronts us. We become "accidental men" by putting our success even in the most important things under the control of circumstances. We get safely across the Rubicon only to begin suffering from a "faint heart," and then a retreat to the rear is the next logical step.

Leaders in particular need to watch this tendency. Real leadership cannot always be stopping to change its plans and directions. If we would succeed, we must make up our minds not only on principles but also on methods. Even the smallest details must be perfectly clear to us. Then we can advance with the firm step of a Caesar determined to conquer our circumstances.

There are very few things that so quickly separate the sheep from the goats or that divide failure from success as this quality of a firm determination to proceed in the right direction.

To improve the quality of our life or of our leadership, we should see to it that no day is allowed to come to its close while any personal conflicts or problems are still undecided. Again, we might get a pretty good idea from Caesar. When Caesar went to capture Britain, he first landed his men and then unloaded his supplies. Then in the night he sent out men and burned the ships in which they had come. Death was now the only Roman alternative to victory. Under such circumstances most men fight with a vigor that never knows defeat. They learn to depend upon their own strength. When we know that we are cut off from outside resources we fight with a vigor equal to the force of desperation. There are many advantages in "burning our ships." When we cut off our chances to retreat, we increase our chances to succeed. Then, like Caesar, once over the Rubicon, there is only one direction to go in, and that is forward.

When starting on an important undertaking, some make the mistake of purposely leaving open a way for retreat. Then, if things get a little difficult, they can always change their minds and their program without embarrassment. But it is not an aid to success to be able to turn back from any point along the way. No one can really accomplish his maximum until he is definitely committed to his task and his mind has closed all lines of retreat. Retreat or surrender should not be made so easy as to actually invite us.

A determined person allows no exceptions to success. Exceptions tear down a success habit faster than victories can build it up. Too often we say, as did the drunken Rip Van Winkle in Jefferson's play, "I won't count this one." "Rip" got into his difficulty because he never really made up his mind.

Most of us, including Rip Van Winkle, know what ought to be done. It is comparatively very simple to write out the formula for almost any accomplishment. But we fail either because we haven't really made up our minds or because we allow too many exceptions. We should make a definite landing and then burn our ships.

Do we really believe the gospel? Have we wholeheartedly accepted our responsibility? Do we know in detail what is required for our particular success? Have we worked out a definite system, including the details of accomplishment?

When any question comes before you for decision, throw all possible light upon it; weigh it in the balances. Then make a decision and go forward. Beware of indecision. Look out for postponements. The temptation toward continual reconsideration is fatal to any forceful action.

One of the greatest thieves this world has ever produced is procrastination, and he is still at large. The indecisive man, the vacillating man, or the procrastinator belongs to whoever can capture him. He is the tool of the last influence that had a chance at him, and just as the driftwood on the river is whirled around by every little eddy and blocked by every obstruction, so the undecided man is spun about by circumstances and other men's opinions. He only marches toward his objective until he gets to the first intersection. If the positive man makes a mistake he will not be long in rectifying it, but the man who never really makes up his mind or is always hesitating, consulting and reconsidering, hasn't much chance to accomplish. This loose-jointedness of will makes continuous effort impossible and distractions deadly. The strong-minded person or the real leader is the one who stands firm in the face of the strongest opposition.

A friend once told me of visiting a certain town the day after

a cyclone had swept through it. Only the solid, substantial struc-
tures were left standing. The weak, rotten trees and the light,
flimsy buildings had collapsed and gone down before the wind. It
is about that way in all departments of life. And the weakest are
always the first to go. A business crisis weeds out the inefficient
businessman. Sickness strikes hardest at those with the least
resistance to disease. The cyclone of sin and failure first removes
from the ranks of leadership the undecided, the unsure and the
undetermined. Only the stalwart and vigorous withstand the
storm.

Testing is a part of our education and training. We must
develop our strength on a crisis basis. Everyday faculties and
abilities are sometimes not strong enough to carry us over the
emergencies. Emergency strength is of a different denomination.
We must have it in readiness. We can't postpone a crisis while we
prepare for it.

God gave man dominion over all things, including himself.
How pathetic to see him crumble like a rotten building before the
storm of some problem or inconvenience! There are no other
qualities that stand so near to genius as a resolute mind and a per-
sistent purpose. These two have won many battles after all other
qualities have surrendered. Great generals say that there is usually
an indecisive period in every battle, an awful moment when the
soldiers are about ready to give up. This is the supreme
"psychological moment" on which everything depends. Then the
courage and faith of the rank and file are ebbing, and the soldiers
feel like running away. These moments sometimes come in every
department of life. Then is the real test. Then is the time when the
leader, for instance, must make the supreme effort to turn the
tide. Workers must be inspired if they are to be kept from break-
ing.

Such an event is told of in connection with the Civil War
battle of the Shenandoah Valley in 1864. The Union troops were
demoralized and scattered. A New York reporter, standing at
that hour upon an eminence overlooking the valley watching the
disorderly retreat, wrote: "I am watching the awful destruction of
the Union." Then a man on a big white horse came racing down

the valley at top speed. He was carrying a pennant with two stars; it was the pennant of the Union general, Phil Sheridan. As he came, he cried, "I am here! Turn about. We will win. We will save the Union!"

It is reported that the men threw their hats into the air and cried like babies. They embraced each other, shouting, "Sheridan is here." The effect was magic. The troops re-formed. By nightfall they had recaptured the Shenandoah Valley. The courage and decisiveness of one man had turned the tide for thousands. Such is the power of a soul with a purpose. Such is your power.

The most hopeful moment in any life is when there comes into it the dawning of a fixed purpose, with definite plans for accomplishment. Then we are able to say, "The die is cast," and we dive into our own Rubicon and with firm strokes head for our destination.

The Glory of the Sun

Some friends of mine recently returned from a trip abroad. Most of their time away was spent in the Holy Land. When they began planning this trip two years ago, they wrote to the steamship companies, airlines, travel bureaus, and libraries for information about the places and peoples they expected to visit. Inasmuch as their special interests centered in Palestine, they had a large map especially prepared on which the places, events, and dates of their particular interest were noted. Then for nearly two years, with the help of some good reference books, they restudied every chapter in the Bible. Upon their return they indicated that this had been one of the most wonderful experiences of their lives. The benefit they had received had been in proportion to the preparation they had made.

With this in mind, let me mention another important journey. In this country we pride ourselves on being extensive travelers. We like to go to new places and see new things and have wonderful experiences. Isn't it interesting, then, to remember that every one of us already has a reservation for the most important and the most exciting trip that anyone will ever make! That trip is when we will take that final journey beyond the boundaries of mortality.

There is a very important similarity between this postmortal journey and some others we are familiar with, in that in each case the benefit received will be in proportion to the preparation made. In fact, virtually all of life is preparation. We prepare for school, we prepare for marriage, we prepare for our life's work, we prepare for death. In the premortal life, we prepared for mortality. In mortality we are preparing for eternal life.

Because of the overwhelming importance of this scheduled journey and the new life it will inaugurate, God himself has provided us with the sacred scriptures to serve us as an authentic guide, a kind of travel literature by which we may prepare for a magnificent experience beyond this life. The gateway to immortality is death, and because we usually think of death as unpleasant, we sometimes fail to make adequate preparation for it. But lack of preparation does not cancel the trip; it just changes the destination.

The school of mortality is like any other school, in that only those who have made satisfactory preparation will receive the highest awards. The scriptures tell us that there is one place above all others that we should plan to attain. The Apostle Paul mentioned this in an interesting letter sent to the members of the Church at Corinth. He indicated to them that they had a choice between three possible destinations, each greatly differing in desirability of the others.

He pointed out that after the Resurrection those who had not "sinned unto death" (D&C 64:7) would be classified into three main groups according to their preparation. He said, "There are also celestial bodies, and bodies terrestrial: but the glory of the celestial is one, and the glory of the terrestrial is another. There is one glory of the sun, and another glory of the moon, and another glory of the stars: for one star differeth from another star in glory. So also is the resurrection of the dead." (1 Corinthians 15:40–42.)

Other scriptures also point out that the most desirable of these kingdoms is the one that Paul refers to as "the glory of the sun." It excels the other kingdoms in glory as the blazing noonday sun excels the soft light of the moon or the twinkle of a faraway star. This is the glory that God himself has instructed us to prepare for. Every commandment that he has given has to do with entrance into the celestial kingdom. The Lord has given no direction about getting into either of the lesser kingdoms. We get into these only by the degree of our default from the celestial.

In this same letter to the Corinthians, Paul said, "Eye hath not seen, nor ear heard, neither have entered into the heart of man, the things which God hath prepared for them that love him" (1 Corinthians 2:9).

We can imagine luxury, elegance, and beauty, costing billions of dollars. In America we speak of our rising standard of living. But who can even conceive of the standard of living in that place where God himself dwells in the "glory of the sun"?

In our own day some wonderful things have happened having a direct bearing on our eternal success. Direct revelations from God have vastly enriched our travel literature and given us far greater knowledge about our own future possibilities. On February 16, 1832, at Hyrum, Ohio, the Lord gave to Joseph Smith and Sidney Rigdon a vision on these three kingdoms of glory spoken of by Paul. He also told them about another kingdom not mentioned by Paul which is not a kingdom of glory. This vision is recorded in section 76 of the Doctrine and Covenants. From any standpoint it is one of the greatest documents in all human literature.

In verses 51 to 53 the Lord tells us exactly how to qualify for the celestial kingdom. He tells us a great deal about what it will be like. There will be no sin there. Celestial glory is the order in which God himself dwells. The glory of God is so great that no mortal in his natural state can live in God's presence. (D&C 67:11-13.)

The Lord has also told us where this glory will be located. After the earth has filled the measure of its creation it will go through a series of changes and find its final destiny as the celestial kingdom. When God created this earth he looked upon it and pronounced it very good. Later the earth was defiled by the sins of its inhabitants. But that curse will be removed, and after the Millennium and the final judgment, the earth will be purified, resurrected, glorified, and celestialized to become the permanent abode of those who have lived here and have qualified for celestial glory. But God has made it very clear that if we desire to live here eternally we *must* be prepared. His exact words are, "If you will that I give unto you a place in the celestial world, you

must prepare yourselves by doing the things which I have commanded you" (D&C 78:7).

This is not just some man's idea. It is the word of the Lord.
He says:

> ". . . he that endureth in faith and doeth my will, the same shall
> overcome, and shall receive an inheritance upon the earth when
> the day of transfiguration shall come;
> When the earth shall be transfigured, even according to the pat-
> tern which was shown unto mine apostles upon the mount; of
> which account the fulness ye have not yet received." (D&C
> 63:20-21.)

On December 27, 1832, the Lord added another important
chapter to our great literature on this subject, known as section
88 of the Doctrine and Covenants. Speaking of the earth, he said:

> For after it hath filled the measure of its creation, it shall be
> crowned with glory, even with the presence of God the Father;
> That bodies who are of the celestial kingdom may possess it
> forever and ever; for, for this intent was it made and created, and
> for this intent are they sanctified.

The Lord has also told us that those who are not qualified
must be cast out. He says,

> And they who are not sanctified through the law which I have
> given unto you, even the law of Christ, must inherit another
> kingdom, even that of a terrestrial kingdom, or that of a telestial
> kingdom.
> For he who is not able to abide the law of a celestial kingdom
> cannot abide a celestial glory.
> And he who cannot abide the law of a terrestrial kingdom can-
> not abide a terrestrial glory.
> And he who cannot abide the law of a telestial kingdom cannot
> abide a telestial glory; therefore he is not meet for a kingdom of
> glory. Therefore he must abide a kingdom which is not a kingdom
> of glory.
> And again, verily I say unto you, the earth abideth the law of a
> celestial kingdom, for it filleth the measure of its creation and
> transgresseth not the law—
> Wherefore, it shall be sanctified; yea, notwithstanding it shall
> die, it shall be quickened again, and shall abide the power by

which it is quickened, and the righteous shall inherit it. (D&C 88:19-26.)

Not only will the earth be celestialized and beautiful, but all who live upon it will be resurrected, celestial personages capable of receiving a *fulness* of celestial glory. Try to understand what you, as a celestial personage, will be like, with quickened senses, amplified powers of perception, and vastly increased capacity for understanding and happiness, made suitable to live in the presence of God.

The Lord says of all such, "These are they whose bodies are celestial, whose glory is that of the sun, even the glory of God, the highest of all, whose glory the sun of the firmament is written of as being typical" (D&C 76:70). But a celestial person is not just a celestial body. The Lord says that the celestial excels in *all* things (D&C 76:92). That means a celestial mind, a celestial personality, a celestial family, and celestial friends.

> They are they into whose hands the Father has given all things—
> They are they who are priests and kings, who have received of his fulness, and of his glory;
> And are priests of the Most High, after the order of Melchizedek, which was after the order of Enoch, which was after the order of the Only Begotten Son.
> Wherefore, as it is written, they are gods, even the sons of God. (D&C 76:55-58.)

What an inspiring portrayal of your possible dignity and destiny!

Now just suppose we don't qualify. Suppose we have paid insufficient attention to our inspired literature in which the Lord is trying to give us direction. Suppose we must then content ourselves with one of the lower kingdoms, with something less fine and far less satisfying. Suppose we are among those that must be cast out, that we must live elsewhere forever, not only away from our family and friends but also excluded from the presence of God. The scripture speaks of outer darkness. It tells of weeping and wailing and gnashing of teeth. Who can understand the depth to which our grief may go when we realize that we have missed the celestial kingdom? The Prophet Joseph Smith said that the greatest misery of departed spirits is to know that they come short of the glory that others enjoy that they could have had. (*History of the Church* 5:425.)

Some of us even in this life have known the intense regret that can come because of a wasted opportunity or some defiling sin.

> Of all sad words of tongue or pen,
> The saddest are these, "It might have been."

The most devastating of all human emotions is the sense of being alone, of being unwanted, of being unworthy. We were born on this earth; we were placed here to get ready; we inherited the right to live here forever, unless through our own disobedience and sin we disqualify ourselves.

But we are still in mortality; we can still qualify ourselves. What a thrilling experience lies ahead if we will only translate the word of the Lord into appropriate preparation! Thereby we will qualify, with our families and friends, to live forever in that wonderful place which has been so aptly described as the glory of the sun.

Keeping Up with the Joneses

Dating back to a time before anyone can remember, a kind of conspiracy has gone on against a particular group of people called "the Joneses." This in spite of the fact that they have probably done more good in the world than perhaps any other group that ever lived in it. Being one of the largest families, the Joneses are mixed in among us so that no one lives very far beyond their influence. Our problem arises from the fact that they sometimes upset our composure when their accomplishments challenge us to adopt a more progressive program for ourselves.

But in spite of all of our moanings and groanings about keeping up with the Joneses, it is still true that a good example from others is one of our most powerful success factors. The Joneses stimulate our imagination by showing us that worthwhile things can be done though they may at first seem impossible to us. The pressure of a good example keeps us on our toes, for which we owe the Joneses a debt of the greatest magnitude.

A magazine article tells the story of a sleepy little village called Brownsville. The homes had a rundown look. The fences were falling apart and the yards were filled with unsightly weeds. But one day the Joneses moved into Brownsville. They bought, remodeled, and painted one of the run-down houses. They cleared out the weeds and built an attractive, nicely painted, white picket fence around the yard. Then they covered the fence with red rambler roses. This greatly upset the status quo that had so long prevailed in Brownsville. It caused a wave of troubled consciences and inferiority complexes to sweep over this easy-going community and made most of the people feel very uncomfortable.

But important consequences soon followed. A good example frequently sets in motion a mysterious force that will not let people rest until the newly discovered virtues are luxuriously growing in their own lives. It was not very long before this uplifting force was transferred to other members of this community. A kind of self-improvement fever started to break out as people began to take a little more pride in their surroundings.

One of the symptoms of what was taking place was the rash of white picket fences covered with red rambler roses that began brightening the face of Brownsville. Some neatly painted houses began to appear, and flower gardens greatly increased in popularity. Some of the people even began paying a little more attention to their personal situation and began to clean some of the weeds out of their own attitudes and personalities.

It was not long before the townsfolk got together, and with considerable community pride and pleasure changed the name of their village from Brownsville to Rosedale.

It has frequently been pointed out that "one man can, if he will, change the morale of a whole community." Thomas Carlyle reminds us that "we reform others when we walk uprightly." It was one of the important teachings of Jesus that man does not live by bread alone. Everyone needs a touch of beauty in his life, and an occasional dose of inspiration helps one to brighten up his outlook and make life more worthwhile. James T. White gave voice to an important feature of this philosophy when he wrote:

> If thou of fortune art bereft
> And if thou hast but two loaves left
> To thee, sell one and with the dole
> Buy hyacinths to feed the soul.

Thomas Carlyle, Jesus, and James White gave this philosophy its form, but it was left to the Joneses to put it in force in the lives of others. Getting ideas into actual operation by example goes far beyond planting flower gardens. It also reaches into the fields of developing good attitudes, a firm faith, and a determined ambition which will build spiritual, social, and financial success.

The story is told of a complacent gentleman who owned a small-town grocery store. Its chief characteristics were the crackel-barrel and the loitering place where certain idle towns-people could sit while they whittled, philosophized, and chewed tobacco. But as the community grew, some Joneses moved into town. They bought the property across the street and there built the most up-to-date building in town. When it opened for business the community discovered that it had a small-scale supermarket with the most modern equipment, the finest stock, and the most effective marketing methods.

The cracker-barrel grocery man stood in his doorway and watched his former customers come out of the new store with smiles on their faces and their baskets filled with groceries. According to his own story, he was the maddest man who had ever lived. He thought the Joneses were robbers who had invaded his territory to steal his business. He felt they were purposely humiliating him in his own community as well as taking away his customers and friends.

After a few months he discovered that getting mad wasn't bringing his customers back, nor was it helping him with his personal problems. It wasn't legal to try to run his competitor out of town or blow up the supermarket. He didn't particularly relish the idea of starving his family or losing his business. Finally, by a process of elimination he decided that the best thing to do was to imitate the vision and industry of his competitor. For the first time he realized that he did not live on the flat stationary earth that people once believed in. It seemed quite unlikely that civilization would soon slow down its pace merely to accommodate his unprogressiveness.

The stimulation he received from these new ideas caused him to take a more honest look at himself than formerly. Then he began taking a new look at the grocery business and at life generally. He gradually became aware that the horse and buggy and the cracker-barrel had gone out of style without his realizing it. He finally came to the conclusion that keeping up with the Joneses had some advantages.

His problem had been so acute and his awakening so real that the pendulum of his ambition began swinging toward the other extreme. In fact, he soon got something resembling an overdose of the spirit of progress, and in the following few years he not only caught up to the Joneses, but he actually passed them. He was cited as the "Grocery Man of the Year" in his community. But what was even more important, he also became an industrious, successful, and happy man in the process.

The power of a good example is one of the most worthwhile forces in the world. Most of us need someone to actually show us the way. We need more and better real live working models of success and righteousness. It is easier to become great in the company of great men. It is easier to become good in the company of good men. It is easier to become successful when we come face to face with the principles of success in actual operation. In more ways that one, competition is the spice of life. It spurs our wills and challenges our ambitions.

There are far too many people who practice the deadly philosophy of defeatism. We are frequently victimized by that terrible disease that sometimes makes failure seem more desirable than success. We need the Joneses to help us clear the cobwebs out of our brains and stir up our spirits. There is far more happiness in victory and success than in defeat and failure. Frequently "it is all in the mind." We think "It can't be done" until we see someone doing it. But even defeatists can't argue with actual accomplishment. Then it becomes a logical step to think that if other people can do great things, why can't we?

Without the influence of the Joneses we are sometimes left sitting around the cracker-barrels of life with no one to show us more worthwhile objectives or better methods of doing things. An example can sharpen our abilities and stimulate our desire to succeed. A little leaven can sometimes make the whole lump worthwhile if we can just get it started to work.

At first everything seems impossible. At one time no one could swim the English Channel. Then Captain Webb did it, then

Gertrude Ederle did it, and since then dozens of others have done it. Until May 6, 1954, no one could run a four-minute mile. But after Roger Bannister had done it, it soon became more or less commonplace for accomplished runners.

This great law of success applies in every field. When one studies the life of Abraham Lincoln it often starts a whole new train of the most worthwhile thoughts in the mind of the student.

I once knew a young man whom I believed to be the homeliest person I had ever seen. He had a great teacher who served him as an ideal. The fact that he wanted to be like his teacher helped him to set his heart on getting a good education for himself. At great sacrifice he worked his way through college and then went east for further training. For a few years I lost track of him and when I saw him again I would not have believed he was the same person. There was an interesting radiance shining in his face and there was a calm confidence in his manner. Success was manifesting itself in every part of his personality. He was no longer homely but was exactly the opposite.

I think of Socrates, who was also noted for his lack of physical beauty. Socrates prayed, "Make me beautiful within," and then he proceeded to answer his own prayer. Socrates planted a flower garden of ideas and ideals in his mind and he became the first one to whom the term *philosopher* was applied. Philosopher means a lover of wisdom. Wisdom and beauty of spirit soon manifest themselves in the personality. The right kinds of thoughts can make the plainest body beautiful. We have all seen plain people transformed by holding beautifying thoughts in their minds and hearts. The working of a radiant personality and a godly spirit transforms our bodies into the likeness of these attributes.

Scripture tells us that even in the resurrection the degree of glory acquired by our bodies will be determined by the quality of our spirits. Only a celestial spirit will be able to resurrect a celestial body. (D&C 88:28-29). Those who have lived the good life will come forth in "the resurrection of the just," and those who have done evil will come forth in "the resurrection of the unjust." (D&C 76:17). So it is also in the realm of the spirit that we are best served by keeping up with the Joneses, since we adopt ideals and develop virtues most readily when we see them in operation in the lives of those we love. This indicates the area of our greatest opportunity, as poverty and riches alike are largely of the spirit. The shiny new automobile in our neighbor's driveway does not stimulate our acquisitive instincts nearly as intensely as does the godliness that shines from the face and personality of an ideal.

Jesus spoke of the power of a great example as a light upon a hill. He instructed his disciples that their lives should be such that men would see their good works and glorify their Father in Heaven. This is a clear-cut case of keeping up with the Joneses. In fact, one of the primary functions of the life of Jesus was to serve as our example. When he said "Come, follow me," he was challenging us to discard our sins and imitate his excellence.

And just think of the effect that his life has had upon those who have followed him. A group of ordinary, unlearned men were transformed by his example into something far greater than themselves, and their wisdom and philosophy is still being quoted after the passage of twenty centuries. Their lives were transformed, for "they had been with Jesus." As they tried to keep up with his example of faith and righteousness, they were lifted toward their own eternal exaltation.

The worship of God is one of our greatest opportunities. As we keep the first and great commandment we bind ourselves to God. As we intensify our worship we immediately elevate the quality of our own lives. It's a matter of following the philosophy that says, "Hitch your wagon to a star, keep your seat and there you are." What wonderful people we could become if we would always keep our wagon hitched to the star of him who said, "I am the way, the truth, and the life" (John 14:6)!

A newspaper article told of a group of astronomers who claimed that their life expectancy had been increased by 20 percent because of their intense interest in such an exalted study as astronomy. But a study of God the Creator is far more important than a study of any of his creations. By putting our lives in contact with him and properly living the gospel that he has designed for our good, we will not only increase the length of our lives but their breadth and depth as well.

The greatest of all objectives is eternal life, and to help us attain it the greatest intelligence of heaven next to the Father himself was sent into the world as the standard of perfection to show us the way and light our path to eternal glory. May we devote ourselves wholeheartedly to living up to this exalted standard.

Scylla and Charybdis

One of the greatest writers of our world was the blind Greek poet Homer, who lived in the ninth century B.C. His primary literary works consisted of two great book-length epic poems. The first is known as the *Iliad*. It is the story of the famous Trojan War.

Paris, a prince of Troy, eloped with Helen, the wife of Menelaus, king of Sparta. Menelaus then enlisted the aid of his fellow kings in the neighboring Greek states. These warriors included the brother of Menelaus, whose name was Agamemnon, a famous Greek fighter who was also king of Mycenae. This assembled aggregation of fighting men sailed a thousand ships across the Aegean Sea and laid siege to Troy, a large and strongly fortified walled city near the Hellespont, in which Paris and Helen had taken refuge. The long war that ensued lasted for ten years, and even then showed no signs of any letup, until by a trick the Greeks finally got inside the city walls. Then in a single night they destroyed the fighting power of Troy, sacked the city, and burned it to the ground. They then loaded their ships and sailed for home.

Homer's second book is called the *Odyssey*. The title is taken from the name of Odysseus, sometimes called Ulysses. He was king of Ithaca and one of the greatest of these Greek heroes. The *Odyssey* is an account of the experiences of Odysseus and his men as they made their way across the three hundred miles of island-dotted sea lying between the battleground of Troy and their home island of Ithaca, off the west coast of Greece.

Odysseus was very happy as he started for home at the head of his own fleet of ships. His men were all delighted that the war was over, and they rejoiced at the thought that they would soon be at their own firesides again with their own families. But in this hope they were doomed to disappointment, for along the way they met with one difficulty after another, many of which were far more destructive to them than the war itself had been. By the time Odysseus finally reached Ithaca every ship had been destroyed and the life of every man had been lost except his own.

This great story about the journey of Odysseus is the grandfather of all adventures stories. Homer knew every trick of getting human interest through storytelling. The *Odyssey* tells of man-eating giants, bewitching sirens, terrible monsters, frightening ghosts, roaring whirlpools, contrary winds, hair-raising adventures, and romantic interludes, not to mention the interest added by Odysseus himself, who was one of the most courageous and ingratiating heroes in all of our literature.

The *Odyssey* has lived in such fine repute through the ages that the word itself has become a part of our language. *Odyssey* has come to mean any long, wandering, difficult journey; and, of course, the greatest of all odysseys is the journey of life itself. We have even come to speak of our strivings for success as an "odyssey," and in the old Greek adventure we find many interesting comparisons to our success in life.

But Homer was not just a great storyteller; he was also a psychologist who looked with keen insight into human lives. In a very interesting way he described the courage, strategy, and super-strength with which these famous heroes tried to solve their problems. He did this in such a way that we are able to receive a substantial benefit from their experiences. Their errors in judgment are made so plain that any repetition by us can be easily avoided. And to be made aware of the moral weaknesses that were so frequently fatal to them provides us with an easy means for our personal escape. Homer's great skill in expression turns his heroes into a reflecting mirror for our own lives. He makes it possible for us to have the advantages from their experiences without suffering any of the penalties.

As Homer describes the problems, longings, and disappointments of his men, and as he tells of the suffering they so frequently brought upon themselves, we are enabled to plan our own lives more profitably by including all that is good in their experience and omitting all that is bad.

One of their most hazardous adventures came as they were required to pass an island inhabited by beautiful, bewitching sirens. It was known that in times past the song of these sirens had lured many sailors off their course to their deaths. Odysseus had been warned about the hazard of listening to the enchanting music of these fascinating, dangerous creatures. As he came near their islands, he feared that his men would not be able to withstand their temptations, and therefore he had all the members of his crew fill their ears with wax so that they would not be able to hear the sirens' songs. Overcome with curiosity, Odysseus himself did not put wax in his own ears. But because he did not quite trust in his own strength to resist, he protected himself against any possible weakness by having his men bind him to the mast. He gave them strict orders that no matter what might happen, they must not release him until they had passed the island and were out of range of any temptation. When they reached the area where they could hear the hypnotic song of the sirens, Odysseus weakened and ordered his men to pull their ship into shore. But their ears were full of wax, and they could not hear his orders. Therefore, this caution of Odysseus saved the day, and they rowed out of range of the temptation with no harm being done.

This ten-year odyssey involved many different kinds of problems. After passing the danger of the sirens, Odysseus was required to run the gauntlet down the narrow Straits of Messina. He must guide his ship between the vast whirlpool of Charybdis on the one hand and a death-dealing monster called Scylla on the other. It is one thing to fight a problem or evade a danger that is all in one place. That is, when one is so afraid of the sirens he can merely either put wax in his ears or give the island such a wide berth that all danger is eliminated. Some difficulties can be averted merely by putting blinders on our eyes. But the problems presented by Scylla and Charybdis cannot be escaped by any such simple means. The narrow Messina Straits made it impossible for the sailors to get a safe distance from one danger without running directly into the other. To close their eyes or plug up their ears would greatly increase the hazard.

Scylla was a frightful female monster with six dog heads, a serpent's body, and many mighty octopuslike arms. She inhabited a rock on one side of the Messina Straits. She would have presented no problem were it not for the fact that directly opposite to Scylla was another monster, called Charybdis, which caused a giant deadly whirlpool in the sea that in the past had dragged many ships and men to their deaths. While trying to escape the danger of Scylla, some had been sucked under by the evil of Charybdis. If the warriors steered a safe distance away from the whirlpool, they put themselves within reach of the octopuslike arms of the monster. And even though every man rowed with his greatest possible skill and the ship of Odysseus barely missed the whirlpool of Charybdis, yet six of his men were snatched from the deck as their craft passed the rock of the terrible six-headed monster, Scylla.

This exemplifies one of our biggest problems in the odyssey called life. Sometimes in trying to miss the evils of one problem as far as possible we run directly into the arms of what may be an even worse problem. Sometimes we resemble a grandfather clock, the pendulum of which alternates in swinging from one extreme in one direction to an equal extreme in an opposite direction.

For example, I have a friend whose marriage failed because of an unbearable weakness in her husband. This particular problem was so impressed in her mind that she developed a loathing for it. To most who knew her, the importance of the problem was far out of proportion in her mind; yet the grievance had been agitated until, like a cancerous growth, it had assumed enormous proportions to her.

Consequently, when this lady got a divorce and began looking for another husband, the one virtue that she sought was the one that her first husband had lacked. She allowed this one quality to so greatly overshadow all other considerations that it made good judgment impossible for her. It was interesting to get acquainted with her second husband. He had the one virtue that her first husband lacked, but that was about all you could say in his favor. He was short in about every other area. He couldn't support her; he had little value as a companion; and as the head of a family he rated fairly close to zero. The reason why her second marriage failed was that she had been so badly frightened by Scylla that she had gone down in the whirlpool of Charybdis.

This is an underlying cause of failure in a great many marriages and a great many other circumstances. Some little sore spot develops in the marriage, and instead of healing up the irritation by reformation and forgiveness or some other kind of settlement, we sometimes pick and scratch at the sore until it becomes so enlarged, infected, and inflamed that it dominates our lives and pushes us into all kinds of problems on the other side of the situation.

One woman sought a divorce from her husband after sixteen years of happy married life. They had had difficulties before, but each time the problem had been resolved and their ship of matrimony had continued to sail a straight and safe course. Then the husband did something that seriously offended the wife. The problem arose at an inopportune time, when tensions were strained and the usual attitudes of give and take were not at their customary strengths. After a flaring of tempers, the wife decided that she would not forgive her husband until he had humbly apologized. This the husband was too stubborn to do, and therefore the apology was not forthcoming. Each held onto his part of the offense with all his heart. As they thought about their problem and picked at their sores, resentments began to grow. The poison got continually greater. The soreness increased, and the dislike became more painful. Each spouse began taking advantage of whatever sanctions were available to him against the other. Then a whole group of problems of incompatibility, frigidity, withdrawal of financial support, lack of communication, and so on, followed in their wake.

The marriage was pushed off its course by a dog-headed,

serpent-bodied Scylla, but their welfare and happiness was completely destroyed in the whirlpool of Charybdis. In trying to steer away from one problem, they had run head-on into several others, each of which was a great deal worse than the original.

I know of one woman who is thinking of getting a divorce because her husband won't let her have her proper say in the handling of the family finances. Another woman is seeking a divorce because she has to take too much responsibility for handling the family's finances. Some wives are unhappy because their husbands are away too much of the time. Others are unhappy because their husbands are home under foot too much of the time.

Most of us resemble the story of the three bears. The papa bear's soup is always too hot, and the mama bear's soup is always too cold. In trying to avoid one horn of the dilemma, we get caught on the other. In rebellion against the left hand, we sometimes go overboard on the right hand. In trying to avoid in ourselves a trait that we dislike in others, we often hurt ourselves by some opposite extreme.

One of the important lessons to be learned in life is to avoid extremes on either side. Jesus talked about the straight and narrow way that leads to the greatest of all destinations, which is eternal life. Like the Straits of Messina, this pathway is very narrow, and no room is left for any meandering or detours. For example, the pathway of honesty is a narrow one. The scriptures themselves are too narrow to accommodate any evil doctrine. The pathway to health is also a narrow one. We need only to get *one* deadly disease in order to die. The path to financial success is so narrow that we can't afford to get off the track too many times.

Those who are troubled with obesity know that the pathway leading to weight control is also a straight and narrow way. It may not be broad enough to tolerate those three pieces of pie.

Success in life is the greatest of all odysseys. And this also requires an ability to be able to effectively run the gauntlet between Scylla and Charybdis. The straight and narrow way leading to eternal life is so narrow that all evil must be left out. It will do us no good to win the greatest Trojan war if we lose our eternal lives on the way home.

We can be outstandingly successful if we remember that the straight and narrow way does not always permit us to do as we please. It is too narrow for immorality and hate and atheism and disobedience to God. There are many things in our lives that must be considered as out of bounds. This is not true of the broad road that leads to death. There anything goes, and everything can be included. It is interesting that no one ever gets off the straight and narrow path at right angles. We merely make the road a little wider so that we can include more of the things that were previously out of bounds.

Jesus indicated that we should put blinders on our eyes and look neither to the right hand nor to the left, keeping our eyes always focused on the objective. If we get even one foot out of bounds on the left, we may get caught by the monster Scylla; and if we get out of bounds on the other side, we may go down to destruction in the whirlpool of Charybdis.

Psychosclerosis

In 1967 Dr. Norman Vincent Peale wrote a very interesting book entitled *Enthusiasm Makes the Difference*. This great word *enthusiasm* comes from some interesting Greek words that signify "God in us." Enthusiasm is that impassioned emotion that gets into people's hearts when they have an inspired interest in some particular thing. It is enthusiasm that gives us an ardent zeal to accomplish. It is made up of a kind of religious fervor causing an exaltation in our feelings.

In his meaningful book, Dr. Peale discusses the importance that a well-directed, intelligent enthusiasm can have in both our material and spiritual success. He also points out some of the many problems that arise when we are not enthusiastic about the right things. When we don't have a sufficient amount of this positive, vital quality in our lives, some of the less valuable negative traits always rush in to fill up the vacuum.

Dr. Peale tells of one occasion when he had an interesting experience with a cab driver in New York City who was lacking something in his enthusiasm for life. As Dr. Peale and two of his friends entered this man's taxi to go to an appointment, they greeted the driver affably and commented on what a wonderful day they thought it was. They asked the driver what he thought about the weather. They inquired about his health, and they asked him how his business was getting along. To each of these genial inquiries, the driver responded with a glum and depressing grunt. It seems that although he was only thirty-five, he had acquired a rather dismal attitude about life generally. It was obvious that he was in a very depressed and pessimistic frame of mind, and this was reflected in his face and had apparently been stamped into his soul.

This situation was naturally very interesting to Dr. Peale, inasmuch as this is the field of one of his special interests. As the conversation progressed among the driver's three passengers there were several occasions when Dr. Peale's friends addressed him as "doctor." This seemed to touch an area of interest in the driver. He logically concluded that he had a medical doctor in his cab and that the occasion provided him with a good opportunity to get a little free medical counsel. Therefore, when a lull in the conversation gave him the chance he was waiting for, he said: "Doc, I wonder if you'd give me a little advice?"

Dr. Peale replied: "Certainly. What kind of advice do you want?"

The driver said: "Well, I haven't been feeling so well lately. I've got a pain in my back, and another one in my side. I don't sleep so good, and I'm always tired, What do you suppose is the matter with me? Do you know of anything you can give me that will make me feel better?"

Dr. Peale is always interested in these kinds of human experiences, so going along with the driver's assumption that he was a physician, he said: "My friend, I seldom practice my profession in taxicabs or give out prescriptions while going along the highway; but since we're both here, I will be glad to give you the best advice I can." He continued: "Of course, you can understand the disadvantages of making an off-the-cuff diagnosis, but it seems to me that you have all the symptoms of psychosclerosis."

This shocking pronouncement so startled the cab driver that he almost ran the cab off the road. It sounded to him as though he had an extraordinary and formidable disease. With considerable concern and apparent apprehension, he said, "What is this psychosclerosis?"

Dr. Peale responded, "Have you ever heard of arteriosclerosis?" The driver was not certain he had, but in any case he indicated that he didn't know what it was.

Dr. Peale explained that arteriosclerosis is a hardening of the arteries, and that any other kind of sclerosis indicated that some hardening process is taking place; that many people have hardening of the arteries, some have a hardening of the nervous system, and others have a hardening of the heart. "But," said Dr. Peale, "what you seem to have is psychosclerosis. That is a condition in which the hardening takes place in the thoughts and attitudes."

That is probably what is bothering a lot of us. It is pretty easy to lose our flexibility, not only in our arteries but in several other places. Some people are suffering from a hardening in their faith or a hardening of their ambition. Sometimes we get hardened in our sins, and some get hardened in their atheism. The doctor doesn't always know the true, ultimate cause of death, so on the death certificate he shows the known physical cause. Actually, many people die because of some hardening that takes place in their point of view.

The taxicab driver was beginning to crack up at this early age in his life because he had lost his enthusiasm. His negative outlook was getting set like concrete, and he had a hardening in his mental attitudes. But out of this taxicab diagnosis Dr. Peale coined a big, imposing, ten-dollar word which might well represent a disease for which more of us should be taking some treatments.

Psychosclerosis is not of recent origin. In one form or another it has been bothering humanity for a long time. We remember the large number of references made in the Bible to those diseases that bothered the Egyptian Pharaoh and brought eleven serious plagues upon his people. Many times Pharaoh hardened his heart while the Lord was trying to get the children of Israel out of Egypt. When the pressure was on, Pharaoh would agree to let the Israelites leave Egypt; but when the emergency conditions relaxed, his unrighteous second thoughts caused a hardening of his heart. The thought of losing this great Israelite labor force not only made the Pharaoh change his mind but also changed his attitudes and put hardness into his heart.

There seems to be a considerable connection between what is in our mind and the condition of our heart. Sometimes when we get our mind set on the wrong things, it hardens the heart toward God and prevents us from doing the right things. But the Lord has his own ways of practicing medicine, and he knows how to go about softening us up. One thing that can help us change our minds and become a little more softhearted is to have some real trouble wherein we undergo some serious suffering. Therefore, when Pharaoh hardened his heart and refused to let the Israelites go, the Lord sent a plague upon Egypt in which the rivers and the other waters were turned to blood. This awful problem caused the Pharaoh to relent for a little while, but apparently the medicine was not strong enough for a permanent cure; and before the Hebrews could get out of the country, Pharaoh had hardened his heart again.

Then, in succession, the Lord sent a total of ten more plagues upon the Pharaoh and the country he ruled. Besides the blood, they had plagues of frogs, lice, flies, murrain, boils and blains, pestilence, hail, locusts, a plague of heavy darkness, and finally the firstborn in every Egyptian family died. Because of Pharaoh's hardheadedness and hardheartedness, much of his country was destroyed. He also lost a large percentage of his people.

But what about us? By hardness and obstinacy in their activities many have brought upon themselves more than eleven plagues and are suffering for about the same reasons that the Egyptians did. On February 27, 1833, the Lord gave us his law of health that we refer to as the Word of Wisdom; and in recent years medical and scientific findings have completely vindicated its principles. Nationally and worldwide many have set their minds and hardened their hearts against these principles, and thereby have brought upon themselves the plagues of alcoholism, lung cancer, emphysema and so on, which have taken many times more lives than all the plagues of Egypt put together. We have also worked up some caffeine plagues, some dope plagues, some plagues of slogan-marchers. We have a plague of sub-reasonable, hard-boiled people trying to force their beliefs onto others. Because so many have hardened their hearts against obeying the law, we are presently suffering some plagues of crime, plagues of vandalism, and plagues of delinquency. We have a tax plague inflicted upon us to pay for the wars and soul sicknesses that desolate our land because as a people we are too hardheaded and too hardhearted to obey either God or our own reason.

When we disobey the laws of God our spirituality gets rigid and brittle and we get mean. Then we become involved with a far worse case of psychosclerosis than the negative taxicab driver had.

The dictionary says that one who is hardhearted is unsympathetic and unfeeling. The newspapers tell of people who have become callous, cruel, and pitiless without even knowing it. The divorce courts tell of people who have become stubborn, willful, and selfish. The scriptures refer to stiffneckedness, ungodliness, and disobedience, which are all varieties of hardheartedness.

Steel manufacturers harden iron by alloying it with other metals. Many of our lives become hard because we alloy them with cynicism, atheism, crime, and sin. When a person's life has been alloyed with evil, the hardness is also stamped in his face and set in his soul. Anyone becomes hard to live with when he is unsympathetic and lacks feeling for the better things in life. Bitterness, immorality, and atheism cause a hardness that can destroy us.

We don't like water that has been hardened by too many impurities. And God doesn't like that hardness in men that makes us incorrigible, inflexible, disobedient, and unloving. The hard heart of Pharaoh brought on the Egyptian plagues, which caused Pharaoh and his people to suffer some very hard times. Likewise our hardness brings hard times upon us. When we have hard hearts, it is hard for us to believe the gospel. And when it is hard to believe the gospel, it is hard to live properly. When it is hard for us to go to church and hard to think right and hard to behave ourselves, it is hard to be enthusiastic or happy or successful. A bad case of psychosclerosis makes us mentally and spiritually gloomy and depressed and probably does us more general damage than any of the other dread diseases.

A man sought psychiatric help who was complaining that the tensions of life were driving him crazy. He was approaching a state of mental imbalance and was not far from a state of hysteria. He kept referring to what he called life's "rat race," and he didn't think that he could endure the tensions of this "dog-eat-dog" world very much longer. He felt he might have to leave town for a while and get away from the tensions that were bringing on his mental breakdown. He had problems in his business; he had marital problems, family problems, financial problems, and personal problems. He felt as though the "breaks" were all going against him. He said that even the air of his town was filled with tensions.

The psychiatrist tried to help him to understand that the tensions were not in the air but in his own mind, heart, attitudes, and nervous system. If one took into the laboratory for scientific analysis and study a sampling of the air from this man's community, it would be found to be absolutely pure so far as any tensions were concerned. It may have a lot of dirt in it or it may have the fumes from airplanes and automobiles. There may even be a little poisonous fallout from our atomic explosions, but not even a speck of tension would be found.

There is no tension in the air, but there is a lot in the people who breathe the air. And we can only have good mental health as we un-tense ourselves and de-confuse ourselves and un-harden ourselves. The scriptural expression "Physician, heal thyself" suggests that we should get the hardness out of our lives. (Luke 4:23).

The Pharaoh could have saved himself from eleven destructive plagues if he had softened his heart and gotten rid of his psychosclerosis. And the most important part of any of our problems is to get our thinking straightened out so that the right kind of attitudes—faith, industry, and righteousness—can flourish in our lives.

When God created us in his image, he also endowed us with a set of his attributes and potentialities. He planted in us all of the seeds of enthusiasm, joy, industry, ambition, and spirituality. All that we need to do is just to nourish them and make them grow. Normal children have a happy childhood, and if they grow up properly their lives will be filled with a healthy excitement and interest in the glory of life. But if we allow too many of the alloys of cynicism, evil, or disobedience into our lives, our viewpoint begins to harden.

It has been observed that the secret of genius is to carry the spirit of childhood over into maturity. That is, it is important to preserve our natural God-given enthusiasm. Jesus said it this way, "Except ye . . . become as little children, ye shall not enter into the kingdom of heaven" (Matthew 18:3). To often we lose unnecessarily this natural enthusiasm for life, which is one of the finest elements of our human nature. If we begin picking up the destructive alloys of selfishness, sin, and disobedience to God, then we start getting psychosclerosis; we become tense and suffer those harmful depressions of the spirit that make troubles hard to endure, success hard to attain, and life hard to live.

Many people die of arteriosclerosis, and a lot more die from the broken hearts, disappointments, gloomy attitudes, and sins that don't get mentioned on the death certificates. A water softener may be a great convenience if we have hard water. But better yet, the philosophy of the scriptures and the Spirit of the Lord will soften up our lives and make us better husbands, better wives, better citizens, and better candidates for eternal life. They will help us to develop our natural God-given enthusiasm for straight thinking and faithful activities, and that enthusiasm will result in health, wealth, happiness, and eternal glory.

The Tree of Knowledge

One of the most interesting stories in sacred literature is recorded in the first part of the book of Genesis. After God had finished the major part of creation, the record says, "out of the ground made the Lord God to grow every tree that is pleasant to the sight, and good for food" (Genesis 2:9). Then the Lord planted a garden in Eden, in the midst of which he planted two special trees. One was the tree of life, and the other was the tree of knowledge of good and evil. Adam and Eve, in their state of childlike innocence, were placed in the garden. The Lord said to them, "Of every tree . . . thou mayest freely eat, but of the tree of the knowledge of good and evil, thou shalt not eat of it, . . . for in the day thou eatest thereof thou shalt surely die" (Moses 3:16–17).

The record continues:

> And when the woman saw that the tree was good for food, and that it was pleasant to the eyes, and a tree to be desired to make one wise, she took of the fruit thereof, and did eat, and gave also unto her husband with her; and he did eat.
>
> And the eyes of them both were opened. . . .
>
> And the Lord God said, Behold, the man is become as one of us, to know good and evil: and now, lest he put forth his hand, and take also of the tree of life, and eat, and live forever:
>
> Therefore the Lord God sent him forth from the garden of Eden, to till the ground from whence he was taken . . . and he placed at the east of the garden of Eden Cherubims, and a flaming sword which turned every way, to keep the way of the tree of life. (Genesis 3:6, 7, 22–24.)

The basic problem in our world is sin. Most of the problems and unhappiness of our lives come because someone has failed to distinguish between good and evil. Life and success in the proper sense of these terms become more and more difficult as we lose the ability to distinguish between right and wrong, or when we come to look upon wrong as acceptable. The reason why God cannot look upon sin with the least degree of allowance is that he understands the deadly effect sin has on people's progress and happiness. We can improve our own welfare as we improve our knowledge of good and evil and understand that evil is no less evil when taken in little doses. Evil is always evil, and it is always harmful. The amount of the dose does not change its nature nor prevent the damage. On the other hand, the most sublime thing in the world, the thing that we should seek after most earnestly, is goodness and truth. Lord Bulwer said, "The truths that we believe in are the pillars of the world." A man cannot be truly great who is not truly good. Atheism itself is merely a denial of God, who is the author of truth and goodness.

In our own interests, we should pay the strictest attention to truth, even in the most minute particulars. Once a deviation from truth is permitted, who can tell where it will end? Or can one be trusted in matters of importance who deserts the truth in trifles?

Someone has tried to compare our knowledge of good and evil to the knowledge of one gathering mushrooms. He said, "If it's a mushroom, you live; if it's a toadstool, you die." It would not show great wisdom to allow even a "few" toadstools among our mushrooms. However, while mushrooms are always mushrooms and toadstools are always toadstools, falsehood may be mixed up with some measure of truth. This makes it much more difficult for us to identify it.

Falsehood and evil are generally rejected when they are seen alone. But when a little evil is sugar-coated with good, the whole pill may be swallowed without our knowing exactly what we are doing.

We have several wonderful safeguards against evil. We have a brain, a conscience, and a great deal of dependable religious instruction. However, our judgment is no better than our information; and to be dependable, our judgment must always be based on facts. It is also helpful if our conscience is never violated or truth ignored. When we allow any exceptions to truth we are deceiving ourselves. When we think one thing and do something else, we become confused and lose our ability and even our desire to distinguish between good and evil. How difficult it can become to reject evil when our own personal interests and pleasures are involved! How much less harmful a wrong course seems that offers a substantial reward! This is especially true if the wrong has enough of good in the mixture to arouse our processes of rationalization. Jesse James made himself believe that he was rendering a community service by bank robbing, since he was taking it from the rich and giving it to the poor. Others believe that they are serving God, when they are actually working for Satan. Many people have blind spots so severe that they can see no evil in themselves or in any of the things they do.

It was suggested to one man that the evil course he was following in his business should be discontinued. The man shrugged his shoulders and replied, "I have to live." His friend's retort was, "I don't know why." How much is even life itself worth if it is characterized by evil? What a pathetic sight to see a child of God whose interest is so centered in himself that he accepts all praise and promise of reward as good, and rejects all criticism and all threats to his personal interests as evil!

Even Jesus was crucified because his teachings conflicted with the unrighteous personal interests of others. But this kind of conflict is also the source of most of our personal sins and problems. It would be a tremendous help if we would eat a little more regularly at the tree of knowledge of good and evil so that we could acquire a more complete objectivity; and if, instead of deceiving ourselves with ridiculous rationalizations and the promoting of our personal self-interest, we could know good and evil as God knows it. Then we would be in a position to begin to make progress. To reach this highest goal, we must never allow evil to pass for good, or good for evil; otherwise, the two will soon come to look alike to us.

Alexander Pope wrote:

> Vice is a monster of so frightful mien,
> As to be hated needs but to be seen;
> Yet seen too oft, familiar with her face,
> We first endure, then pity, then embrace.

There are no "necessary evils." True success and true happiness are never built on wrong. Character and righteousness are the most genuine manifestations of genius. It does not require a strong character to be dishonest. The easiest thing in the world is to lie and cheat. But the man in the greatest demand by either material or spiritual success is the man who can always be trusted. He is the one who can and does make a sharp differentiation between right and wrong. He is the one who would rather be cheated than to cheat. He would rather suffer wrong than do wrong. And those people who are continually making mistakes because of their ignorance are not much better off than those who make the same mistakes because of their folly. Most men fail in business and in life because they stumble and fall over such wrong things as dishonesty, immorality, sloth, lethargy, failure to keep the Ten Commandments or to follow the Golden Rule, or simply the inability to tell right from wrong. It is a handicap to success to be more interested in what is expedient than in what is right. Sometimes we put opponents, sinners, and problems all in one package labeled Evil. Then, with some rationalization such as "I have to live," we put friends, personal advantage, and our own interests in another package that we label Good. Our knowledge of good and evil deteriorates through lack of desire or postponement on our part.

In Robert Louis Stevenson's story, "The Master of Ballantrae," the young aristocrat was asked why he was such a rascal although he was so well versed in the scriptures. He answered, "The malady is that of not wanting." What a deadly malady it is not to want goodness and honor and God! What a terrible disease possesses us when we postpone good or train ourselves to love evil merely because we are favored by it! We should hate evil in any combination or location.

One loses his ability to make clear distinctions between good and evil by calling the same things by different names under different circumstances. The "sin" that we see clearly in others so frequently looks like "helpful experience" when it shows itself in us. But if any sin is too much indulged, even under a false name, it gets us so involved that we may soon lose the power to change our course.

We must learn to recognize and love truth, no matter from whence it comes. And the greatest homage that anyone can pay to truth is to live it. The way to develop a love of truth is to work at it. Neither good nor evil can be contained within prescribed limits. When we live truth, it spreads to others. Evil does the same thing. One of the most horrible tragedies in life is that we so easily satanize each other. When Lucifer walked out of heaven, one-third of all of the hosts of heaven followed him. But the same thing happens with us: When we do some evil thing the contagion quickly spreads to others. Down the roadway of life no one walks alone; each stands at the head of some kind of caravan.

To indicate the profound influence of example, we might study our trends in modern art, or in women's hats, or in the good or evil conduct of groups. History shows that people tend to move up and down the moral scale together. It goes in periods—like the Dark Ages, the Reformation, the age of invention, or the age of evil.

In the book of Helaman, the following is recorded: "And in the commencement of the sixty and seventh year the people began to grow exceedingly wicked. . . . they began to set their hearts upon their riches; yea, they began to seek to get gain that they might be lifted up one above another." (Helaman 6:16-17.) It would appear as if all of these people got the idea at about the same time. No doubt they said, "Everybody's doing it." Acceptance of a bad example is one of the most destructive ways of dulling our sensibilities and making evil seem right to us. Then we become so confused by our false standards that we lose the ability to tell right from wrong.

Someone, probably in an attempt to be facetious, said that George Washington couldn't tell a lie. Then he named someone else who, he said, couldn't tell the truth. But the most pathetic characterization was reserved for the poor unfortunate who couldn't tell the difference. It is a common weakness that "when reason is against a man, the man will usually turn against reason." We turn against the Church and against God not because they are wrong but because we are wrong.

The communist leaders have set their minds on dominating the world, not because that is right but because it seems to them to be in their interests. Because their ambitions are contrary to God and the Bible, they banish God and the Bible from their land and close up the church by governmental decree. They are interested in deceit, force, murder, and even world destruction, because these things seem to best serve as instruments of their selfish design. To break their own agreements or violate their own promises are all perfectly proper to them if their purposes are served.

Right and wrong for its own sake seems to be a concept unintelligible to power-mad dictators.

But we may also lose our way as individuals for the same reason, and instead of being able to distinguish between right and wrong, our distinction may be made between what is profitable or unprofitable, pleasant or unpleasant. We cannot pursue even a good end by evil means without sinning against our own souls. God is the only absolute guide as to what is right or wrong. He is the North Star by which we must square our lives with truth, not only on Sunday but every day in the week. What good does it do to run after a sermon on Sunday if we lie and cheat during the week? It is extremely perilous to try to separate right thinking from right acting, and he is already half false who studies truth but does not live it.

When man became mortal, access to the tree of life was placed temporarily beyond his reach to prevent him from living forever in his sins. Fortunately for us, there is no flaming sword presently guarding the tree of knowledge of good and evil, and every one of us may eat to his heart's content.

What Shall I Do with Jesus?

During that long, awful night of betrayal and trial, Jesus was brought before Pilate. Pilate believed Jesus to be innocent of any wrong and made a weak attempt to save his life by taking advantage of one of his privileges as Roman governor to release one prisoner to the Jews at the time of the Passover.

Pilate had in his custody a noted insurrectionist and murderer by the name of Barabbas. Probably relying upon the sense of fairness of those accusing Jesus, assuming that they would not consent to the release of a notorious criminal and punish an innocent man, Pilate said to them, "Whom will ye that I release unto you? Barabbas, or Jesus which is called Christ?" (Matthew 27:17.) Pilate must have been startled to hear them shout, "Barabbas." He asked, "What shall I do then with Jesus?" and they replied, "Let him be crucified" (Matthew 27:22). Pilate said, "Shall I crucify your King?" And they answered, "We have no king, but Caesar" (John 19:15).

Then Pilate took water and washed his hands before the multitude, saying, "I am innocent of the blood of this just person: see ye to it." And they said, "His blood be on us, and on our children." (Matthew 27:24–25.) Barabbas was released, and Jesus was delivered to be crucified.

We might safely assume that both Pilate and the Jews felt they had permanently settled any question which might arise in connection with the life of Christ; Pilate by merely washing his hands, and the Jews by putting to death the very Son of God. But there is a peculiar relationship which exists between the life of

Jesus Christ and every other person born into the world. What Pilate and the Jews did that night did not in the slightest alter that relationship—either for them or for us. Inasmuch as Jesus also bore our sins, we are also party to his death and cannot escape our share of guilt. That is, it was our sins as well those of his contemporaries that made it necessary for Jesus to volunteer his own death. In addition, we are assured by Peter that "there is none other name under heaven given among men, whereby we must be saved" (Acts 4:12).

Our salvation is determined by the way we decide certain important questions. James Russell Lowell spoke of this responsibility under the title of "The Present Crisis."

> Once to every man and nation
> Comes the moment to decide;
> In the strife of Truth and Falsehood,
> For the good or evil side;
> Some great cause, God's new Messiah,
> Offering each the bloom or blight,
> Parts the goats upon the left hand
> And the sheep upon the right.
> And the choice goes on forever,
> 'Twixt that darkness and that light.

Certainly the greatest question to be decided by anyone in the world is the question asked by Pilate when he said, "What shall I do with Jesus?" The Jews made their decision by saying, "His blood be on us, and on our children." The question is still before us, and each must answer for himself.

> For Jesus is standing on trial still,
> You may be false to him if you will;
> Or, you may serve him through good or ill;
> What will *you* do with Jesus?
> You may evade him as Pilate tried,
> Or you may serve him whate'er betide;
> Vainly you'll struggle from him to hide;
> What will you do with Jesus?
> What will you do with Jesus?
> Neutral you cannot be.
> And someday your soul may be asking,
> What will he do with me?

One of the best methods for solving any problem is to carefully weigh each of the alternatives. In this particular case there seem to be three possibilities. The first method for solving this problem is to follow the example set nineteen hundred years ago and reject Jesus. As the Apostle Paul points out, we may thereby "crucify . . . the Son of God afresh" (Hebrews 6:6). Such a course deliberately taken is unthinkable. But much of what the Jews did they did in ignorance.

Upon the cross Jesus said of the Roman soldiers, "Father, forgive them; for they know not what they do" (Luke 23:34). Those who crucified Jesus didn't really understand the awfulness of their deeds. Pilate did not even know who Jesus was. But why didn't he know? There is only one possible answer, and that is that he had not invested the time and the effort and the thought necessary to find the truth. Pilate could have found out who Jesus was, just as any one of us can find out who Jesus is if we are only willing to make the necessary effort.

Pilate indicated a common technique for evading decisions when he said to Jesus, "What is truth?" (John 18:38.) And then without waiting for the answer he turned and walked out of the room. That is about the way we sometimes investigate the gospel. We may know the truth if we search for it diligently enough; for only those who fail to seek fail to find. But the religion of Jesus has always suffered more at the hands of those who didn't understand than from those who have deliberately opposed. This is also our greatest source of personal danger.

That is, almost all of the sins of our world are the sins of ignorance. Most of those who violate the commandments of God don't really know the importance of what they are doing. When we fill our minds with evil thoughts, we seldom understand until it is too late that these ideas will determine our eternal destiny. Even the highly educated Saul of Tarsus was guilty of this great sin of ignorance. He referred to himself by saying, "Who was before a blasphemer, and a persecutor, and injurious: but I obtained mercy, because I did it ignorantly in unbelief" (1 Timothy 1:13). When Paul went to Athens he found many people ignorantly worshipping before the unknown God (Acts

17:23). That sin is still common among us. We should beware of the sin of ignorance. It is the basic problem even in our world of education and enlightenment.

The second alternative for the proposition of "What shall I do with Jesus?" is that we may try to be neutral. That is, we may try to be neither one thing nor the other. Of course, that is impossible, for either God is or God is not. There is no middle ground. It is all or nothing. If we don't accept him by design, we reject him by default. When we fail to decide a question one way, we automatically decide it the other way, just as when we fail to decide to get on the train, we automatically decide to stay off the train.

A man who does not openly declare his loyalty to Christ is probably no better than a mere onlooker, or what someone has described as an "inquiring neutral." There is a large group of people who say they *do not believe,* but they also say that they do not disbelieve. It has been pointed out that there is one folly greater than that of the fool who says in his heart that there is no God, and that is the folly of him who says he doesn't know whether there is a God or not. The skepticism of one who does not believe is not so hopeless as the skepticism of one who does not care. Unbelief is often a mere confession of lack of interest and the unwillingness to investigate.

When we are unwilling to fight for a thing, we may frequently soon find ourselves fighting against it. Neutrality in faith always means defeat in accomplishment. It is frequently our faint hearts rather than our sinful minds that stand between us and our eternal exaltation. Nor can we merely brush the question of Jesus aside in unconcern. One of the most destructive sins in our world is the spiritual inertia of otherwise good people. It is easy and dangerous to assume rather than to investigate.

If a person should err in believing the gospel of Jesus Christ to be true, he could not possibly be the loser by the mistake, but how irreparable is his loss who should err in assuming the revelations of God to be false! There are a great many people who try to dispose of this question, "What shall I do with Jesus?" by saying that he is merely a great teacher. This is also a very unsatisfactory substitute for a personal testimony of the truth. Someone has said:

> Suppose there is a Christ, but that I should be Christless,
> Suppose there is a cleansing, but that I should remain unclean;
> Suppose there is a Heavenly Father's love, but that I should remain an alien.
> Suppose there is a Heaven, but that I should be cast down to Hell.

"It is impossible for a man to be saved in ignorance" (D&C 131:6), but it is also impossible to be saved in indecision.

Our third alternative for the question, "What shall I do with Jesus?" is that we may accept him for what he claimed to be, the Son of God and the Savior of the world. On the occasion of his baptism, then on the Mount of Transfiguration, then during his visit to the Nephites, and again in our own day, the voice of God the Father has been heard saying, "This is my beloved Son, in whom I am well pleased." (Matthew 3:17, 17:5; 3 Nephi 11:7; Joseph Smith—History 1:17.) What greater authority could we have to accept Jesus eagerly and serve him enthusiastically? What a great privilege we have to fill our minds with the commandments of God and consecrate our lives to his service!

Ralph Waldo Emerson indicated our problem: "On the brink of the ocean of life and truth we are miserably dying. Sometimes we are furthest away when we are closest by. We stand on the brink of an ocean of power, but each must take the steps that would bring him there."

Frequently we are furthest away when we are closest by. Those who lived contemporaneously with Jesus were near. Jesus lived among them. They saw him pass along the street; they heard him speak; they knew of his miracles; but in their lack of sufficient investigation they pronounced sentence upon themselves by rejecting their Redeemer. Now we are near. We live in the greatest age of enlightenment ever known in the world. We see the wonders of God on every hand. We have what the Jews had, but in addition we have the judgment of time shining upon the life of Christ. We have the testimony of the apostles, who gave their lives to put it in force. But in addition, in our own day the gospel has been restored in a fulness and clarity never before known in the world.

Fervent and convincing testimony has been borne to us that in the early spring of 1820 God the Father and his Son Jesus Christ reappeared upon the earth to reestablish among men a belief in the God of Genesis, the God of Calvary, and the God of the dispensation of the fulness of times. And we are given the means whereby we may acquire a personal testimony for ourselves. There are now available for our study three great volumes of new scripture outlining in every detail the simple principles of the gospel. They give God's answer to the greatest question of our lives, the question that will determine our eternal destiny. Pilate's question has come before us anew. "What shall I do with Jesus?"

"We stand on the brink of an ocean of power, but each must take the steps that would bring him there." If these steps are not taken, it may mean that we also are far away—far away from the ocean of power that is Jesus Christ.

The Buck Stops Here

For many years President Harry S Truman kept a sign on his desk which said, "The Buck Stops Here." This phrase gets its meaning from what someone has said are the three American traditions—one is the passing of the Indian, another is the passing of the buffalo, and the third is the passing of the buck.

There is a disabling human weakness that sometimes causes people to try to sidestep their problems and shift the responsibility to someone else. It is easy just to say: "Let George do it," "That isn't my job," or "Why should I stick my neck out?"

As an intended solution to our problems, many of us just pass the buck. That is a process of refusing the effort and denying the responsibility. Then it is a short step to developing the habit of blaming other people or charging up our failures to conditions. For our failures we blame our family or our education, or we sometimes feel that fate itself is against us. Very frequently people blame their sins and weaknesses onto something that happened in their childhood. One says, "Because my parents made me go to church when I was young, I have never been religious since I have grown up." One man said, "The reason why I am not successful is that my father was not a pusher." By many and varied processes we learn this irresponsible art of "passing the buck."

Frequently, when someone gets a little droopy or discouraged or prematurely tired, we try to put a little more life into him by telling him to "buck up." That means to take heart, to brace oneself with a stronger courage reinforced by a greater industry. To "buck up" means to brighten up, to get smart, to dress up, to think in bigger terms, and to attack life's assignments a little more enthusiastically.

If any of us should analyze ourselves, we might possibly discover that too much of our time is spent in this sinful pastime of "passing the buck." We could greatly help if we would follow the philosophy of President Truman and firmly say to ourselves "The buck stops here." I am not aware of all of the things that the president may have had in mind, but certainly when one becomes the president of the United States, he is at the end of the line, and there is no one that he may pass his problems on to. He has been elected by the people and is expected to solve all those problems for which he carries the responsibility. His official advisors were all appointed by him. In the event of their failure they may be removed from office and someone else appointed in their places, but the president is elected and must answer to the people. While he is in office he is a kind of committee of one. His heavy responsibility cannot be passed on to anyone else. It cannot be delegated. If the president abandons his duty, then the power is lost, for no one else receives authority merely because the president may be idle or unwise or derelict in his duty. Ordinarily, the president is all alone and is a very lonely man.

When the atomic bomb became a reality, the United States was at war with Japan. Thousands of American lives were being destroyed by an aggressor nation that had initiated a war by a sneak attack upon our military outposts. President Truman had been elected to be the Commander-in-Chief of our armies and was the only man who could decide whether or not the atomic bomb should be used on our enemies. If it were not used, the war would continue and thousands of additional American lives would be lost. On the other hand, he knew the consequences of using this terrible, destructive power. But the decision *must* be made, and the buck stopped at the desk of Harry S Truman.

President Truman also had other momentous decisions to make. One of them was to relieve of his command a very popular general by the name of Douglas MacArthur. General MacArthur had proven his ability and loyalty to his country many times. Mr. Truman knew that his contemplated action would bring upon him a great avalanche of criticism from those millions who almost worshipped the famous general. How the president must have wished for someone else to whom he could pass this unpleasant responsibility! As this problem was weighing so heavily upon him, he must have looked pretty hard at that little sign on his desk which said "The Buck Stops Here."

In spite of the fact that General MacArthur had better training in military procedures and knew far more about winning wars than did President Truman, the president was the only human being in the world who had the authority or the responsibility to decide the question, and he must live forever in his country's history with whatever criticisms might come from his decision. All buck-passing must stop at the desk of the president.

And while most of us will never be president, each of us also has an important job to do and each of us must carry the complete responsibility for his own task. This usually requires about as much courage, initiative, industry, punctuality, and actual ability as we are able to muster.

During the Civil War, an energetic color-bearer carried his company's flag a little too far ahead of the troops. The captain called out to the color-bearer to bring back the colors to the line. The color-bearer shouted back what he thought was a better idea. He suggested that the captain bring the line up to the colors. We must also keep ourselves up with the colors, and there is no one to whom we can pass the buck for that responsibility.

There are many disadvantages to this practice of passing the buck, and it is quite likely that some of us could profitably use a similar card on the desks of our own lives, saying, "The Buck Stops Here." Each of us is his own commander-in-chief. And each of us has the responsibility for keeping our accomplishments up with our colors. Every situation in life carries its own responsibility, and each of us has been elected to be his own man. There is no place in life at which we can afford to accept the position and then deny its obligations. When a person is born into this world of privilege, he is also obligated to accept his share of its work. When God said to man, "Thou mayest choose for thy-self," (Moses 3:17), man was not only made his own commander-in-chief but was also saddled with the full responsibility for his choices.

There is an interesting phrase used many times in the scriptures in which some people are referred to as "the elect of God." The earth is the Lord's and the fullness thereof, and every person born into it has a calling that amounts to an election for which he must answer to God. The duties of our mortality are not easy to sidestep, and they certainly cannot be ignored. To begin with, God created this earth for our benefit, and he has never given a law without also giving a corresponding set of conditions to go with it. It is interesting to remember that not all of God's children were permitted to come to this earth with physical bodies. Satan and the one-third of the heavenly hosts that followed him were rejected as candidates for mortality. But those who won the election must also assume the obligation, and "the buck stops here."

No one can do our deciding or our growing or our repenting for us. Certainly no one can carry our responsibility for us, and no one can sidestep the consequences of his own deeds. The Lord has indicated that we should take upon us his name. We should also square our shoulders for that load of responsibility for making this earth a proper place to live. The Apostle Paul said that each of us is responsible for working out his own salvation in fear and trembling before God (Philippians 2:12). In substance, Peter was writing out a card for our desks when he said to all Church members: "Wherefore . . . brethren, give diligence to make your calling and election sure" (2 Peter 1:10). He was laying the responsibility directly upon us when he said: "And beside this, giving all diligence, add to your faith virtue; and to virtue knowledge; and to knowledge temperance; and to temperance patience; and to patience godliness; and to godliness brotherly kindness; and to brotherly kindness charity" (2 Peter 1:5-7).

When President Truman took office, he also took an oath in which he said: "I do solemnly swear that I will safely execute the office of president of the United States, and will to the best of my ability preserve, protect, and defend the Constitution of the United States, so help me God."

But God has provided an oath of office for each of us, and he laid the responsibility right on the line when he said, "He that believeth and is baptized shall be saved; but he that believeth not shall be damned" (Mark 16:16). We also have other obligations. Once each week we partake of the emblems of his sacrifice, and each week we covenant that we will always remember him and keep the commandments which he has given us. One would be ill advised if he tried to pass off that responsibility, as the consequences of such a choice will last forever.

For four years President Abraham Lincoln carried the same responsibility that President Truman did, and during the bitter years of the Civil War he said that many times he was driven to his knees because he had nowhere else to go. If we were looking for a better solution, where would *we* go? God is our judge, our lawgiver, our highest court of appeal, our only city of refuge, and our only hope of reward.

In the days of Jesus some of the people created a serious problem for themselves by this process of ignoring their responsibility. Of those who were offended by Christ's doctrine the record says that "From that time many of his disciples went back, and walked no more with him. Then said Jesus unto the twelve, Will ye also go away? Then Simon Peter answered him, Lord, to whom shall we go? thou hast the words of eternal life. And we believe and are sure that thou art that Christ, the Son of the living God." (John 6:66–69.)

If we sidestep that responsibility our alternate choices are extremely limited, for to whom can we go? To whom can any of us turn if we lose God? So far as the affairs of our eternal lives are concerned, "the buck stops here," the decision is ours to make, and there is no one to whom we can pass the buck.

One of the most necessary elements in any bid for eternal success is to learn the art of being responsible to God. That responsibility makes our need for right moral decisions an absolute necessity. To live at his best the man created in God's image must have nobility, righteousness and dependability, and must be able to carry his own affairs forward effectively. To be responsible, a person must be competent, solvent, honest, capable, reliable, and trustworthy, so as to be able to discharge all his debts to God and his fellowmen. When we put all of this on our own card and then sum it up it says "The Buck Stops Here."

Real responsibility allows no alibiing, no excusing, no rationalizing, no procrastinating, and no shirking. No one else can be held accountable for our dishonesty, or our indecency, or our negative thinking, or our lack of spirituality, or our failure in actual good works. No one can be asked to be decent for us, or honest for us, or constructive for us.

Franklin D. Roosevelt once tried to explain how Russia got along with other nations, and he said, "Of course, Stalin is an awful liar." From the very first, communist philosophy has been built on lies. The brutal communist takeover in Hungary, as well as their ruthless maneuvers in Czechoslovakia and East Germany, were all based on false claims, but they had thousands of tanks and guns to back up their treachery. And so it has continued. In their newspapers, in their public pronouncements, and before the United Nations they have made all kinds of buck-passing misrepresentations which everyone knew were untrue. A young boy with a similar philosophy was once asked who started the fight in which he was involved. He said: "Bill started it when he hit me back." We put ourselves in a similar situation when we blame circumstances and events for our evil instead of ourselves.

The communists are professional liars and professional buck-passers, and we cannot take their word as a responsible expression. But *everyone* who tries to deceive is irresponsible. What is our situation when we lie to life and to God and to ourselves? When we become aggressors in evil and life punishes us, we often feel as if we are being unfairly treated. But when anyone breaks any of the Ten Commandments or any other divine law, he must answer to God for his irresponsibility. God has given no one the *right* to do *wrong*. It is our *privilege* to do wrong, but because it is not our *right,* we must always expect to suffer the consequences.

In every activity we should take our own oath of office before God with a pledge to do right. Whether our goals lie in social, educational, moral, financial, or spiritual fields, we ought to say to ourselves, "The buck stops here." Under God, each of us is his own commander-in-chief, and we should pray that God will help us to be fully honest, fully righteous, and fully responsible.

The Land of the Book

On the first Thursday of each month I have the prized privilege of sitting with other General Authorities of the Church in a sacred meeting held in an upper room of the Salt Lake Temple. The chairs are arranged in a semicircle facing the First Presidency. It is in this upper room that the leaders of the Church have held many of the most important meetings since the days of Brigham Young. It is a great thrill to realize that in times past some of the greatest men of this dispensation have met in this room as they have considered important matters relating to the upbuilding of God's kingdom upon the earth. And always lying on the table near the center of the room are the four books of holy scripture that are referred to as the standard works of the Church, books containing the word and the will of the Lord.

It is a stimulating fact that many of the ancient prophets had much of their attention focused on the present age. Isaiah's visions and prophecies made him seem almost to live in our time. Both Isaiah and Micah seem to have seen the Salt Lake Temple itself as they looked forward to our time and said:

> And it shall come to pass in the last days, that the mountain of the Lord's house shall be established in the top of the mountains, and shall be exalted above the hills; and all nations shall flow unto it.
>
> And many people shall go and say, Come ye, and let us go up to the mountain of the Lord, to the house of the God of Jacob; and he will teach us of his ways, and we will walk in his paths: for out of Zion shall go forth the law, and the word of the Lord from Jerusalem.

And he shall judge among the nations, and shall rebuke many people: and they shall beat their swords into plowshares, and their spears into pruninghooks: nation shall not lift up sword against nation, neither shall they learn war any more. (Isaiah 2:2-4. See also Micah 4:1-3.)

The ancient prophets knew also many of the details about our great present-day knowledge explosion. Isaiah could only have been speaking of our modern airplane when he said, "Who are these that fly as a cloud, and as the doves to their windows?" (Isaiah 60:8.)

The prophets seemed to shudder a little as they beheld the wars and rumors of wars that they saw us bringing down upon ourselves. They worried about our lawlessness, hates, weaknesses, and sins, some of which may never be corrected until the glorious second coming of Christ when our earth will finally be cleansed of those problems with which we are burdening it. From some points of view our age has a rather questionable reputation in history. Jesus himself made an unfavorable comparison for us when he said, "But as the days of Noe were, so shall also the coming of the Son of man be" (Matthew 24:37).

We have a helpful proverb, however, to the effect that God always sends the remedy before the plague. A long time before our latter-day plague of problems began, God had prophets write down some effective cures for those diseases with which we are presently afflicted, and these writings appear in the Holy Bible. This volume of scripture is easily available throughout the world, yet we are not getting nearly as much good out of it as there is in it.

Of course the Bible itself was not known in the original Bible lands, and in the days of Christ his message was largely met with rejection and apostasy. In the years following his crucifixion his apostles were slain, and Jerusalem, the headquarters city, was also soon destroyed. The people presently occupying the original Bible lands are not primarily Christians, and the Bible has never been readily accepted there. The Bible as we know it grew up largely in Britain.

In 1604 King James I of England appointed a group of fifty

scholars to select the manuscripts for the Bible and to translate them out of their original tongues and make them available in the English language. In the year 1611, after seven years of work, the scholars published the present King James Version of the Bible. This is also called the Authorized Version, and on its title page is a statement saying, "Appointed to Be Read in Churches." The Bible soon reached a place of great popularity in Britain.

Victoria became the queen of Great Britain in 1837, and during her sixty-four-year reign the British Empire grew to include over a fourth of the entire globe. Britain also became the world leader in science, trade, colonization, commerce, and culture. Britannia ruled the waves and the sun never set on her possessions. It is small wonder that this important nation came to be called *Great* Britain.

Victoria was frequently asked to explain the unparalleled success of her nation. As a reply she would always place her hand upon the Bible and say, "Britain is the land of the book." Victoria accounted for her country's greatness and prosperity by the fact that her people as a whole honored the teachings of the Bible. And as long as Britain lived by the book, the nation prospered. But conditions changed, and the nation released its hold on important Christian ideals. The great empire has crumbled. And as Britain has declined as the land of the book, she has also declined in her influence, culture, prosperity, and power.

In this changing process, Providence has passed the Bible over to America. There is indisputable evidence that God superintended the discovery of this continent and raised up our Founding Fathers to establish here this great democratic nation to be the citadel of liberty and to serve as his chief national advocate of Christianity.

Many centuries before Columbus, an angel showed an ancient American prophet a vision of the United States as a young, growing nation. The prophet describes a part of his vision by saying: "And it came to pass that I, Nephi, beheld that they did prosper in the land; and I beheld a book, and it was carried forth among them. And the angel said unto me:

Knowest thou the meaning of the book? And I said unto him: I know not." (1 Nephi 13:20–22.) Then the angel told the prophet that this book contained the will of the Lord and the covenants which the Lord had made with the house of Israel. He made clear that this book would be a very important factor in determining the future destiny of the nation he had shown Nephi in vision. Thus from its very beginning the United States of America, like Britain at some time, has been the land of the book.

Our system of government was created by God for the benefit of everyone upon the earth. America has a great mission to perform, not only for herself but for every person in the world. This would be a far different world if there had never been a United States of America.

One of the most precious possessions of our world is its holy scriptures. The Bible is the world's first book of religion. It is the world's first book of wisdom. If fully followed, it would guarantee our religious, our military, our material, and our national success. We should constantly pray that this great natural resource will be widely read, fully understood, and adequately lived by every American citizen. The proper use of the Bible, effectively supplemented by the other standard works of the Church, would guarantee a glorious success for everyone who would follow this course.

Only when we follow the word of the Lord can we expect the peace, prosperity, and happiness for which we have such great need. The Psalmist gave us an important and everlasting "law of the book" when he said, "Blessed is the nation whose God is the Lord" (Psalm 33:12). This corresponds with the question asked of us by one of our prominent Founding Fathers, Benjamin Franklin, when he said, "If a sparrow cannot fall to the ground without his notice, is it probable that an empire can rise without his aid?" He gave us the answer when he said, "I believe that without his concurring aid we shall succeed in this political building no better than the builders of Babel." God is presently telling us that we are blessed when we live by the great principles of eternal success written in the book.

Some major purposes of the mission of the Son of God

were to teach us the sanctity of life and the importance of governments, and to establish his church upon the earth. Of course, he desires that we govern our lives by the principles of righteousness. He organized his church in Palestine in the meridian of time, and from this Asiatic center the message of the gospel later was sent out over much of the world. The Savior was crucified, and after his ministry in Jerusalem the resurrected Lord himself took his church to the people on the American continent. On both continents, however, it would eventually be destroyed by sin. The black night of apostasy set in, followed by the centuries of the Dark Ages. On the eastern hemisphere, the Savior's apostles were slain, and the church Jesus established in Palestine splintered into hundreds of unauthorized fragments. In fulfillment of his divine promises, however, on April 6, 1830, the original Christian church was restored to the earth in the state of New York. It is now operating on a basis as nearly worldwide as possible.

Instead of being a world of just one book, the world now has four sacred books of holy scripture to help us solve the increasing number of modern problems. Each of these books becomes a part of and supports the others. Our age is the period which Paul looked forward to and called "the dispensation of the fulness of times," when all things in Christ, both those in heaven and those on earth, should be gathered together in one (see Ephesians 1:10). This applies particularly to our holy scriptures.

These four great volumes of scripture point out our greatest opportunities to live by God's divine command. He wants us to govern our lives by these standard works of his church. All of these books become one book for our guidance and direction.

God has granted many great blessings to America. We have a great governmental system, great wealth, great power, great education, great scriptures. This is the land of the book. The headquarters of the Church is here. With all these great blessings we also have great responsibilities. We ought to again review the question put to the prophet, "Knowest thou the meaning of the book?" (1 Nephi 13:21.) And then we should make sure that we know the right answer, for the extent to which we live by the book is still the most important factor in determining our destiny.

We cannot escape the fact that we are the land of the book, and the greatest opportunity of our lives is to live its teachings. And if we magnify our callings, we can help every person in the world to achieve his full destiny as a child of God. May God help us to be successful.

Frankenstein

In 1818 Mrs. Percy Bysshe Shelley published a novel called *Frankenstein.* The story is centered around a young medical school scientist who is specializing in chemistry and anatomy. He had been a party to many interesting discussions in and out of the medical school about the possibility that man might some day be able to create life.

Young Frankenstein was a little over-impressed with the idea, and accepted this scientific challenge as his own project. He worked long and hard until he was finally successful. He discovered that tremendous secret which for so long had been hidden from the understanding of men. In the period that followed, he gathered from the dissecting rooms, the morgues and other available places the necessary parts and materials. Then in his laboratory he built a huge male monster in which he housed the life he had discovered.

His creation was of fearsome appearance. It had long ragged hair, rolling blood-shot eyes, and ugly yellow features so distorted and loathsome that no one could look upon them without a scream of terror. But this creation also had a set of loathsome emotions, which were inherent in the parts from which it was made. Being virtually lacking in moral sense, it committed numerous atrocities and crimes. Its depraved nature cut it off from any friendly association with mankind, and it was not long before this hideous giant had declared a personal war against the entire human species. Above all it determined to be avenged upon the man who had formed it and sent it forth in its unbearable misery.

One by one, either through violence or through grief, this creature brought about the deaths of all the members of Frankenstein's family, as well as all of his dearest friends and his bride. From the first, Frankenstein himself lived a life of deep remorse. He was not able to stop nor to destroy the monstrosity that his hands had fashioned. After Frankenstein's own death had been brought about, his evil monster disappeared into the northern seas.

Mrs. Shelley, the author, lived to know that she had added a new word to the English language. The word *Frankenstein* is now a synonym for a man who by his own creation brings disaster or destruction upon himself. Inasmuch as Frankenstein's monster itself bore no name, the name of its creator has sometimes been transferred to it. Therefore in popular usage "a Frankenstein" has also come to stand for some being of appalling ugliness and brutality, one having all the beastly evils of mankind and lacking in man's godly moral sense.

There is something about this fanciful tale that runs true to human nature, and the word *Frankenstein* therefore has almost become a common noun. The story rings a kind of bell in our own experience. Like Frankenstein himself, most of us set forces in motion that turn and hound us forever.

A century ago Emerson gave a voice to our Frankenstein tendencies when he declared that "things are in the saddle and ride mankind." If Emerson felt this way in the conservative New England of his time, what would he think of our present-day world? Certainly man, the producer, is now being ridden by his product. The machine which man intended to be his tool, frequently becomes his tyrant. It puts him out of work or runs him down on the highway. We sometimes create wealth, only to have it turn on us and give us stomach ulcers and nervous breakdowns. Governments are built by men with the intention that they will serve as our tools and servants. But often, like Frankenstein's creature, they get out of hand and rise up to deprive their creator of his property and even his life itself.

The governments of Stalin, Hitler and Castro tyrannize over people and have actually destroyed the lives of millions to whom they were intended to bring peace and security. We see another fearful Frankenstein in the great bomb which we spent so much time and effort to create. It is now threatening to turn upon us and wipe out our civilization. But like Frankenstein the scientist, we also build up individual Frankensteins to personally tyrannize over us and destroy the best in our lives. Throughout our land we have built up many liquor distilleries in which we brew up that awful monster that rides our highways to cripple, maim, mutilate, and destroy. This Frankenstein of alcoholism causes many of our crimes and brings upon us much of our poverty, dishonesty, and immorality.

Mrs. Shelley got the idea for her novel from a terrible nightmare. She tried to reproduce in her book all its terrible aspects and preserve all its terror. She said she wanted to communicate to others the mysterious fears and dreads of our nature and thereby awaken an awareness of the awful horror that can occupy human hearts. If Mrs. Shelley was horrified by the ugliness and destructive ability of the eight-foot monster of her nightmare, what would she think of that alcoholic demon that has brought so much misery and unhappiness to so many people!

One example might be cited of a beautiful mother of three children who for the last sixteen years has never left her bed because her car was smashed by a Frankenstein speeding down the highway while his brain was crazed with alcohol. She is only one representative of the thousands of innocent people whose lives, bodies, and spiritualities have been mutilated, degraded and destroyed by this ugly beast that man has created and set against himself.

There are respectable people who under the title of social drinking turn loose upon the world a thousand Frankensteins. I know of a great business leader, who like the creator Frankenstein, has the very best of intentions. He furnishes excellent leadership for his company. He desires to be helpful to his employees. But in representing his company, he frequently makes occasion to get his employees and associates together for what is called a social hour. Dressed in evening clothes with good friends and enough free liquor, drinking can be made to seem fashionable, pleasant, and even profitable. Under the pressure of his Frankenstein this man himself is fast becoming an alcoholic, but he is also helping his friends to form a habit that does more damage to the bodies, minds, and spirits of men than a million Frankensteins. The great God of creation has said that the day will come when every man must be judged according to his works. He must also be judged according to the influence he has had in the lives of others.

The greatest power in the world is the power of example, that is, the way we learn to walk and to talk. That is the reason why we speak with the particular accent we do, the way we select our clothes and determine our hairstyles. That is the source from which we get our manners and our morals. That is also how we acquire our sins and our bad habits. Carlyle said, "we reform others when we walk uprightly." But we also destroy others when we set them a bad example. Down the broad way of life no one walks alone; each one stands at the head of some kind of a caravan. We cannot avoid the responsibility for those we lead.

I have always been impressed with the ability and function of the bellwether sheep. He leads the flock out to the pasture and then back home again. He wears a bell to let the owner know where his sheep are.

Some meat packers got the idea of capitalizing on this natural leadership by training the bellwether into what is called a Judas goat whose job is to lead the sheep into the slaughterhouse. After leading his sheep companions into the slaughtering pens, he escapes from the trap through a private door. Then the sheep are butchered, while the Judas goat goes back for another trusting group. There are many who in one way or another resemble a Judas goat at the slaughterhouse. Through their influence they lead other people to destruction by helping to popularize what Robert G. Ingersoll once referred to as "that damned stuff called alcohol."

Mr. Ingersoll says that alcohol demoralizes everyone who touches it from the time it issues from the poisonous worm of the distillery until it spews itself out upon the world in crime, immorality, poverty, dishonesty, disability, and death. It corrupts the one who makes it, the one who advertises it, the one who sells it, the one who drinks it, the one who helps others to develop a taste for it and make its use seem fashionable and pleasant. There are many employers who would fire an employee who was ten dollars short in his accounts, yet these same employers permit, and themselves foster, this slaughterhouse tactic of the social hour. By their influence and approval they help to create a thousand Frankensteins to ravish and destroy the lives and homes of their fellow human beings. If confronted with their guilt, they frequently repeat in shocked surprise the words of the first murderer, who said to God "Am I my brother's keeper?"

Of course, alcoholism is not the only bad habit we create to tyrannize over us. One man said to his wife that he thought he would stop smoking. To his great surprise she expressed regret that he had not done so years earlier before *she* had taken up the habit to keep him company. She was now a chain smoker, unable to quit. Like the Judas goat in the slaughterhouse, this good man has led his own wife into a trap from which she is now unable to free herself. Isn't it interesting that most of the habits that destroy our lives come from our best friends. Very few people would ever give liquor or nicotine or profanity the power to tyrannize over them, if it were not for the example of some bosom friend.

The size of the Frankenstein is not important. He may be the Russian leader with his fingers on the button of the bomb, or he may bring about the fearsome destruction of alcoholism by playing the part of the Judas goat among his social or occupational friends. But whatever our lives may be, we cannot escape the responsibility of our influence. Every human being must someday stand before God in judgment. Even the lowly hobo must be responsible for the life he drags down with him. As John Donne said, we are all involved in mankind.

In Dickens's *Christmas Carol* the miserly Scrooge is confronted in a dream by the ghost of his dead partner Jacob Marley. Marley, like Scrooge, had been a hard, stingy, money-grubbing, selfish individual during his life, and now from the realm of the departed his spirit comes back in self-condemnation. He warns Scrooge against the fate toward which he is also directing his own life. As the ghost wrings his hands and bemoans his sorry state, Scrooge tries to console him by saying, "But you were always a good man of business, Jacob." At this, Marley's ghost cries, "Business, business, mankind was my business, the common welfare was my business, charity, mercy, forebearance, benevolence, were my business!" Too late Marley had discovered that he was also involved in mankind, and that the real business of life was helping to solve the problems of human beings. Putting together Frankensteins or turning destructive influences loose upon the world should not be our business.

To be destructive the Frankenstein doesn't need to be a monster eight feet tall with blood-shot eyes and horrible countenance, whose fearful form fills us with horror. Such a demon is less dangerous because its approach is more easily detected and we are warned to be on our guard. As in the case of many an alcoholic, we may suffer far more serious damage from those smaller, more pleasant Frankensteins, who with happy countenances go on their errands of destruction dressed in evening clothes.

I know of a great leader who has position, ability, money, success, and many wonderful traits of character to recommend him. Yet in his ordinary speech he profanes the sacred name of Deity many times a day. Because of his many good qualities he tends to make this ungodly sin seem smart and respectable to others. Yet no matter how smart it may seem to some, it is displeasing to God, and he has given his word that "the Lord will not hold him guiltless that taketh his name in vain" (Exodus 20:7). But even when we stand before God, our Frankensteins will be on hand as our accusers. A great passage of scripture says: "For our words will condemn us, yea, all our works will condemn us . . . and our thoughts will also condemn us; and in this awful state we shall not dare to look up to our God; and we would fain be glad if we could command the rocks and the mountains to fall upon us to hide us from his presence" (Alma 12:14).

Every sin and every bad habit has the nature of a Frankenstein, and once they are given life, they will follow us to hell and will use every opportunity to turn and rend the one who brought them into being. May God help us to deliver ourselves and our friends from evil by devoting our lives to righteousness.

Collectors

The most interesting of all subjects for study, contemplation, and improvement is ourselves. And yet we probably know less about ourselves than any other thing. If someone were to ask us questions about science, invention, or history, we could answer them, but if they asked us to write out an analysis of ourselves and tell them about our mind and soul qualities, we may not give very good answers. For example, why is it that we do as we do, when we believe as we believe?

We don't know very much about our premortal past, or how much, if any, of it has carried over into our present. One of the most important things to be remembered about ourselves is that we are children of God, formed in his image, and endowed with a set of his attributes. We should also keep in mind that we are heirs to God's glory, and through a divine growth process the obedient offspring of God may hope to eventually become like the parent. To help us realize our fullest potentialities, we are born into this life with certain natural tendencies, and one of the most meaningful of these is what someone has called the "collecting instinct." Without any special instructions or education, we all start out in life as collectors.

To demonstrate this natural law, suppose you turn any small boy upside down and shake him a little bit. You will probably find that a whole collection of colored rocks and broken glass, marbles, chalk, pieces of string, and an occasional chicken foot will drop out of his pockets. Then if you set a detective on his trail, you will also discover some pack-rat characteristics as he leads you to a cache of valuables he has stashed away without knowing why. As this boy becomes older, he will upgrade the quality of his collection. He will possibly get possession of a dog, a gun, and a fishing pole. If the subject of your study happens to be a girl, you will find that her collection includes dolls, dishes, handkerchiefs, and dresses. She will also have a hope chest filled with all kinds of accumulated treasures.

These collecting abilities all seem to be in the human package as standard equipment at birth. Inasmuch as these tendencies are presents from the Creator, we assume that they were meant to serve a good purpose, and that he intended us to develop them and direct them into the most productive channels. As these fundamental abilities are being enlarged, we begin collecting incomes, savings accounts, real estate, life insurance policies, and stocks and bonds. But a very fundamental part of this acquisitive instinct is directed toward the collecting of knowledge, abilities, virtues, and skills. We collect friends and memories.

Jesus was trying to stimulate our collecting activities in the right direction when he said to his apostles, "Seek ye first the kingdom of God and his righteousness, and all these things shall be added unto you" (Matthew 6:33). The kingdom of God is sometimes thought of as "a place" or "an organization," but it has also been referred to as "a condition." Jesus said to one group of people, "the kingdom of God is within you" (Luke 17:21). There is a note in the King James version that says that he meant "the kingdom of God is among you," and that may be what he did mean. But it may also be true that the kingdom of God is within you. Certainly faith, courage, and determination can only exist inside of individuals. In fact, it doesn't really matter very much what is ahead of you or what is behind you, because all of the most important things are inside of you. When Jesus mentioned "God's righteousness," he was thinking of something that should get inside of us. For before any of us can get into the kingdom of God, it is necessary for the kingdom of God to get into us.

Someone once said that it doesn't help a person very much to go through college unless the college goes through him. One might be baptized into the Church every twenty minutes with little avail unless he gets the Church into him. Jesus mentioned "talents" and "things," and we should remember that "things" always follow "talents." If we can collect enough "talents," the "things" will come as a natural consequence. That is, when we have collected an effective combination of education, industry, attitudes, skills, and habits we are pretty well on our way to any projected success.

It is very important that good collectors should also be wise discriminators. Otherwise we may someday discover that we have an assortment of such wrong things as headaches, distraught nerves, weak wills, vain regrets, bad reputations, tobacco breaths, and cancerous lungs. Bad men are most easily distinguished from good men by the kind of habits they have stored away in their personalities. Even the finest collecting instinct may backfire and become a liability unless the person possessing it quickly discards those things that are undesirable. A fisherman catches all kinds of fish in his net, and he may occasionally get a turtle or an octopus; or, to change the figure, we might compare our success to success in the mining industry. Before ore has value it must be run through the refinery. A good smelting operation is one that efficiently retains the gold and discards the dross.

It is a general rule in life and in mining that no ore comes pure. And the place of discrimination and good judgment in life is to help us to separate the good from the bad. Then we can take the gold into our life's treasury and throw the dross away. For this same purpose farmers use combine harvesters to separate the chaff from the wheat. The chaff is thrown away and the wheat is put in the bin. A good conscience and a sound reasoning ability are life's threshing machines.

When God created us as he did, it was his thought that as we moved through our world of opposites where good and evil were growing side by side, we should save the wheat but discard the tares to be burned. In agriculture or in life, we are not likely to find many fields where some tares are not inclined to grow among the wheat. Throughout the universe there are disease and health, right and wrong, success and failure, growing side by side, and over all God has erected a sign saying, "Thou mayest choose for thyself." This collecting instinct with its powerful urge to acquire is indispensable to success, but it is just as necessary that we also develop our ability to discard.

A good fisherman may throw back everything he doesn't want. It is not necessary for a miner to go through life burdened down with the dross. A farmer is not required to put the chaff in the bin. And one of the greatest privileges of life is that we may throw back anything that would bring discord or ugliness to our lives, yet we may collect the good things to our heart's content. It is a great idea to collect stamps, autographs, butterflies, silverware, tapestries, or paintings. It is wonderful to own land, build barns, develop factories, and store up goods. We may select the occupation offering us the highest challenge, the finest opportunity for service, and the greatest reward of money in the bank.

What a thrilling idea it is that in addition we can acquire the most satisfying collection of abilities, virtues, character qualities, and personality traits! We also have the inestimable privilege of selecting a life's companion and collecting a family of capable, righteous children who in turn are good collectors. Because the primary compensations of our lives depend upon our skills as collectors, we should decide as early in life as possible what it is that we want to collect. Suppose, therefore, that we make up our own individual collection list.

I suppose that in a place of high priority we would have a notation to collect and hoard as much good health as possible. It is reported that John D. Rockefeller, the world's first billionaire, offered to give his chauffeur half of his wealth if the chauffeur would change stomachs with him. If a good stomach is worth a half a billion dollars, what would a sound heart, a clean mind, a good pair of lungs, a stable nervous system, and a righteous soul be worth?

In February 1833 the Lord gave to the Prophet Joseph Smith a revelation that is recorded in the eighty-ninth section of the Doctrine and Covenants. The Lord said that tobacco, liquor, tea, coffee, and some other things were not good for us, and that it is pleasing to God when his children abstain from using them. Just think how many billion-dollar lungs, how many billion-dollar hearts, how many billion-dollar minds, and how many billion-dollar nervous systems could be saved if we had the good judgment to obey God and discard all our evils. Some of the most important parts of our religion are the "thou shalt not's" of the Ten Commandments. For when our minds are definitely settled about those things that we *don't* want, then we can effectively begin to collect those things that we *do* want.

Only when we have definitely decided that we don't want ignorance are we in the best condition to obtain a good education. The first thing that Adam and Eve were asked to decide after they were placed in the Garden of Eden was whether or not they would eat the fruit of the tree of knowledge of good and evil." After they had eaten, God said, "Behold, the man is now become as one of us to know good and evil" (Moses 4:28). And I would like to point out in passing that the right kind of knowledge still tends to have that effect upon people. It still tends to make man become as God is.

In addition to our many opportunities in formal education, we also have a limitless number of good books filled with a wealth of wisdom and inspiration. God has not only honored us with the privilege of choosing for ourselves, but he has arranged a vast inventory of knowledge from which selection may be made. And we may collect to our heart's content. If the chauffeur's stomach was worth half a billion dollars to John D. Rockefeller, how much would Abraham Lincoln's honesty be worth to us? But without any expense we can include in our collection of virtues the integrity of Mohandas K. Gandhi, the determination of Winston Churchill, the courage of Joan of Arc, the manhood of George Washington, the wisdom of Ralph Waldo Emerson, the fairness of Benjamin Franklin, the industry of Thomas A. Edison, and the religion of Jesus Christ. We can collect a reverent spirituality, a thankful heart, a loyal devotion to right, an effective ability to do good, a sound understanding of the gospel, and a deep appreciation of the finest things in life.

What an exciting possibility that we may also increase the value of our collection with a virtuous heart, an enthusiastic attitude, a cheerful personality, a willingness to serve, and a set of the finest habits!

Some of our material things are subject to the law of diminishing returns. An increase in financial wealth sometimes has a decreasing ability to serve our needs and make us happy. For example, John D. Rockefeller may not have been ten times more happy with ten billion dollars than I would be with one billion. Riches are not always what they seem to be to those who don't have them. Emerson once said, "I would that everyone was rich that he might know the worthlessness of riches."

It is unwise to devote too much time or energy to something that does not bring a corresponding return. Jesus gave us an idea for a vastly increasing rate of return when he suggested laying up for ourselves treasures in heaven. Treasures in heaven have many advantages. They are more satisfying and a lot more permanent. William James once said that the greatest use of life is to spend it on something that outlasts it. The real value in collecting is to collect those treasures that will last forever. In this connection it is interesting to remember that poverty and riches alike are largely of the spirit. Someone pointed out one of the shortcomings of earthly riches by saying, "You can't take them with you." And someone else has added that, with taxes as they are, you can't even keep them while you are here.

Another weakness of earthly riches is that they are not negotiable in that realm where we hope we are going to spend our eternal lives. Suppose, therefore, that we follow this more profitable suggestion of laying up treasures in heaven and center our attention upon the religion of Jesus and his program for our eternal progression. The greatest of all of our human concepts is the immortality of the personality and the eternal glory of the human soul. Throughout eternity you will be yourself and I will be myself, with quickened senses, amplified powers of perception, and vastly increased capacity for reason, understanding, love, and happiness, all of which are qualities we may develop now. Our machines wear out, our barns fall down, and our substance goes back to the dust, but our finest collection of personal qualities will have eternal life. The wonders of personality are so unlimited that we even think of God himself in terms of them.

Real wealth is not so much what we have as what we are. We don't work merely to acquire, but to become. Success in life isn't just what you can get out of it, but it is what you can become by it. Jesus said, "He that hath eternal life is rich." Stamps, butterflies, stocks, mortgages, and real estate may sometime lose their value, but our treasures in heaven will continue to provide us with success and happiness forever. May God help us to lay up those treasures and thus make the most of our wonderful collector's instinct.

America the Beautiful

A number of years ago Eugene Burdick and William Lederer wrote a book entitled *The Ugly American*. This title represents an attitude some people have about Americans and America. Many of us do not present the most attractive picture of ourselves, and it is natural that ugly activities in Americans will reflect unfavorably on the American image.

In recent years a deterioration in our conduct has seriously impaired the elegance of our reputation and the effectiveness of our success. This fact has more than ordinary significance in view of the large amount of evidence that this great nation was established by the direct design of God on a foundation of freedom and righteousness. Each individual citizen is obligated to bear his fair share of responsibility not only for his country's political image but also for her social, moral, and spiritual welfare. The great empires of the past have fallen because of the ugliness that was allowed to become a part of their national inheritance. And while to some it may not seem very important what Mr. Burdick and Mr. Lederer may think about America or any other people, every nation must rise or fall according to the image it presents in God's sight.

Some time ago a woman in a divorce court described what it was like to be married to an ugly American. For twenty-nine years her husband had scoffed at religion. He had dominated her every move and had denied her many of her normal liberties, including her freedom to worship and to live a righteous life without being humiliated and made to feel that she was something less than a human being. Her husband assumed the privilege of depriving his wife of her right to go to church. Because of his high affinity for the deceit and misrepresentation that he felt would be helpful to him she had lost all of her confidence in his sense of fairness and integrity. He set his children an ugly example through alcoholism, nicotine addiction, profanity, atheism, and extreme antagonism toward God. He was not only an ugly American; he was an ugly Christian, an ugly husband. For twenty-nine years his wife had submitted to his evil in an unsuccessful attempt to win a "peaceful coexistence" of right and wrong in their home. As a consequence, the lives of all the family members had become distorted with evil and all were molded more or less into the father's moral image.

If we sing "God Bless America" as criminals and delinquents, we should not expect that God will answer our prayers very enthusiastically. After God had finished his work of creation, he looked out upon the world and called it very good. Certainly God, who sees the end from the beginning, provided the unmatched fertility of our soils, our great rivers, our magnificent forests, our lakes of oil, and our mines filled with valuable metals, with a desire to bless the people who would live here. He wants to build a beautiful America, filled with beautiful Americans and beautiful Christians.

The word *Christian* was first used in Antioch to designate the followers of Christ, and Christianity is one of the characteristics of America. Our nation was built on Christian principles, and our present and future success depends upon Americans following the Master. One cannot be a great American without having the qualities of Christian beauty in his life.

While standing in one of the garden spots of America, I once tried to imagine how many billions of buckets of paint God must have used to beautify our mountains, our landscapes, our homes, and our flower gardens. Our red apples, yellow peaches, purple grapes, blue plums, black cherries, and many-colored flowers impress us with the fact that God loves color and harmony. We might also wonder about the billions of "buckets" of perfume, taste, and nourishment that he has skillfully put into the flowers, fruits, and other things to delight the senses of man. But God reserved his greatest beauty to put into his own children inhabiting every land and nation. And while there are many variations of ugliness in Americans, there are also many whose lives are filled with beauty, human dignity, and voluntary righteousness.

God promised to spare the little city of Sodom if fifty righteous men could be found therein, but there must be many more than that number of righteous lives to account for the great lavishness with which God has blessed America. America is beautiful for her freedoms and for her stable government. America is beautiful for her lack of blood purges, gas ovens, dictatorships, and political revolutions used by so many nations as the instruments of government. America is beautiful for the sacred regard for human life and human dignity that is written into her Constitution. America not only has the largest number of people claiming to be Christians of any nation but also the largest percentage of church attendance. America sends out more religious missionaries and makes a far greater effort to help other people economically than all the other nations in the world combined.

Our national flag represents a way of life that is the envy of the world. As we pledge our allegiance to that flag and to the republic for which it stands, we vow our wholehearted support to this greatest nation under God, which *he* has made indivisible in order to more effectively provide liberty and justice for all. Our national motto declares that it is "in God we trust," and so far as we practice this motto, our land will be free and our lives will be successful. It is much more than a coincidence that for almost two centuries we have remained free amid the great turmoil and slavery besetting other nations. Someone has said that in America it is "believe it or not," whereas in so many other countries it is "believe it or else."

Many years ago Katherine Lee Bates wrote a poem that reflects the spirit of America. It is entitled "America the Beautiful." And inasmuch as the successes of America and Americans are so dependent upon each other, we might weave in between the lines some sentiment about those beautiful Americans who, under God, have helped to make America great.

> Oh beautiful for spacious skies,
> For amber waves of grain,
> For purple mountain majesties
> Above the fruited plain!
> America! America!
> God shed his grace on thee
> And crown thy good with brotherhood
> From sea to shining sea.
>
> Oh beautiful for pilgrim feet,
> Whose stern impassioned stress
> A thoroughfare of freedom beat
> Across the wilderness!
> America! America!
> God mend thine every flaw,
> Confirm thy soul in self-control,
> Thy liberty in law.
>
> Oh beautiful for heroes proved
> In liberating strife,
> Who more than self their country loved,
> And mercy more than life!
> America! America!
> May God thy gold refine
> Till all success be nobleness,
> And every gain divine.
>
> Oh beautiful for patriot dream
> That sees beyond the years
> Thine alabaster cities gleam,
> Undimmed by human tears!
> America! America!
> God shed his grace on thee
> And crown thy good with brotherhood
> From sea to shining sea.

It must be pleasing to God when we love our country and try to build up her great institutions. America should be a place where "follow the leader" of righteousness is not a game but a way of life. We can develop our own appreciation by reminding ourselves of the many benefits that we enjoy as well as the many obligations that come to us as a consequence of living in this highly favored, free land.

What price would be too great for American freedom and American opportunity, or who could do too much to keep these blessings alive and vigorous in our land and in our hearts!

During the first century of our national existence Abraham Lincoln said: "We have been the recipients of the choicest bounties of heaven. We have been preserved these many years in peace and prosperity. We have grown in numbers, wealth and power as no other nation has ever grown." Then he mentioned our perennial problem when he said:

> But we have forgotten God, we have forgotten the gracious hand that preserved us in peace and multiplied and enriched and strengthened us, and we have vainly imagined in the deceitfulness of our hearts that all of these blessings were produced by some superior wisdom or virtue of our own. Intoxicated by unbroken success, we have become too self-sufficient to feel the necessity of redeeming and preserving grace, too proud to pray to the God who made us. It behooves us then to humble ourselves before the offended power, to confess our national sins, and to pray for clemency and forgiveness.

Abraham Lincoln was speaking as the president of the United States, but he might have said those same things if he had been speaking as a prophet of the Lord. We feel the spirit of the prophets as we hear President Lincoln say:

> Whereas it is the duty of nations as well as men to own their dependence upon the overruling power of God, to confess their sins and transgressions in humble sorrow, yet with assured hope that genuine repentance will lead to mercy and pardon, and to recognize the sublime truth, announced in the holy scriptures and proven by all history, that those nations only are blessed whose God is the Lord; and inasmuch as we know that by his divine law, nations, like individuals, are subjected to punishments and chastisements in this world, may we not justly fear that the awful calamity of civil war, which now desolates the land, may be but a

punishment inflicted upon us for our presumptuous sins to the needful end of our national reformation as whole people?

If only those nations are blessed whose God is the Lord, then above all we must continue to serve him.

America is beautiful. And she can become the most beautiful nation in her repentance and in the reformation of her national life. Our society will always have problems as long as some of us continue to show ourselves as ugly Americans or ugly Christians.

And we must do far more than follow the Master merely with our lips; our hearts also must be beautiful. We must have God's doctrines clearly in our minds, and we must keep all of his commandments. We would like to be well regarded by other nations, but it is far more important that we be on good terms with the God of this land, who is Jesus Christ.

On each anniversary of our nation's birth all Americans should join together in expressing their appreciation for the greatness, goodness, strength, and beauty of America. As we repledge our love, loyalty, and support, may we ask God to help us be good Americans and good men and women; for only as Americans are good can they be beautiful, and only as they are beautiful can they be free.

A Great Time to Be Alive

Years ago Harry Emerson Fosdick wrote an interesting book entitled *It's a Great Time to Be Alive.* He pointed out some of the miracles and wonders that make our age the most exciting since creation. In the United States we enjoy the highest standard of living ever known in the world. In a material way, we live better than any king lived just a hundred years ago. Any one of us would count it an incredible hardship to have to live as Solomon lived in all his glory.

However, I suppose *any* time is a great time to be alive. The American writer Henry Thoreau said we should thank God every day of our lives for the privilege of having been born. Then he went on to speculate on the supposition of what it might have been like if we had *never* been born, and he pointed out many of the blessings that we would have missed as a consequence.

What Mr. Thoreau may not have known was that one-third of all the spirit children of God never were born and never can be born, because under the leadership of Lucifer they rebelled against God in their premortal state and forever forfeited their right to a physical body. They must continue eternally as Satan and his angels, with all their opportunities for growth and happiness cut off. Some of these unembodied evil spirits appeared to Jesus in his day, preferring the bodies of swine rather than to have no bodies at all.

I am sure that if we understood the eternal importance of the body we would prefer having the most broken, twisted, unsightly body to having no body at all. We would have preferred to live in the most benighted, backward times, under the most unfavorable conditions rather than not to have lived at all. How great our gratitude should be to live in the most important age in the greatest nation, under the most favorable conditions ever known in the long history of human life, to live in a day when we may have all the education we desire!

We live in a day when the knowledge of medicine helps to give us strong bodies and clear minds. Since George Washington's day our life expectancy has been exactly doubled, but the length is not the only dimension of life that has been increased. There has also been an improvement in its breadth and its depth; and yet no one is satisfied.

The only kind of life that is permanently satisfactory is eternal life. God holds out the promise that if we live according to his directions, we may someday qualify to eat the fruit from the tree of eternal life. God has said that his greatest gift to us is eternal life, and he has made clear how it may be attained.

Jesus announced his own mission by saying, "I am come that they might have life, and that they might have it more abundantly" (John 10:10). Life is the greatest commodity in the world, and it is the one thing over which God himself has maintained exclusive control. With all our boasted wisdom and science, no one has ever yet been able to produce even a single life cell. The greatest combination of scientists cannot make even one live kernel of corn. All of the medical men in the world put together are unable to produce one live red corpuscle. But God's ultimate objective for us is that someday we may merit the thrilling blessing of an exalted, eternal life. This is the kind of life that God himself has. God has designed and ordained a natural development process for us called eternal progression. If we follow his plan, the offspring of God can eventually become like the parents.

Our life's purpose is not just to live long but to live interestingly, constructively, and well. Success in life is not just what we can get out of it but what we can become by it. Branch Rickey, the famous baseball manager, was once asked what was his greatest day in baseball. He said, "I don't know, I haven't had it yet." And certainly our greatest days are those that we haven't yet had.

Our present lesser days provide the time to prepare for our greater future days. The best use of mortal life is to exchange its energy and discipline for something more important and more permanent. The tragedy of our world is the unpleasant fact that most people have traded their mortality for some mere fraction of life rather than the eternal abundance mentioned by Jesus. Frequently we actually use our time here to bring misery and unhappiness upon ourselves for both here and hereafter. Jesus himself compared our sinfulness with that of those people who lived in the days of Noah. In the creation of our giant crime waves, our vandalisms, and our moral decadence, we are effectively imitating the antediluvians who brought a watery destruction upon themselves. Yet in spite of our serious delinquencies, the scriptures still foretell a very bright future for our earth and those who may qualify to live upon it eternally.

After God had created the beautiful paradise called earth, with its peace and plenty, he called it very good. Then came the fall of man and the accompanying curse upon the earth. Deserts and waste places began to appear; a destructive enmity developed involving both man and the beasts. The status of our sphere was lowered from a terrestrial to a telestial rank. During the some six thousand years since that time, our earth has operated in its fallen state. It has continually brought forth thorns, thistles, and noxious weeds, while sin and wickedness have flourished upon its face. At the end of the six thousand years, corresponding to the six days of creation, the earth's Sabbath will begin. It will be initiated by the second coming of Jesus Christ to cleanse the earth of the unhappiness and death that have been its chief characteristics.

At the second coming of Jesus Christ, while the earth is being cleansed by fire, those who are ripened in iniquity will be destroyed. The governments of the earth will be replaced by the perfect rule of Christ, who will reign as King of kings and Lord of lords for a thousand years.

During this millennial period, both mortal and immortal

people will live upon the earth. The earth itself will be raised to the status of a terrestrial sphere, and it will again be a beautiful paradise, as it was before man's sin placed the curse upon it. What a great time this will be to be alive! Then those who have survived the cleansing will live in peace, and their children and grandchildren will grow up in righteousness. Their bodies will be immune to disease, and their minds will be filled with health and vitality. Ignorance will be done away with and the knowledge of the Lord will cover the earth, even as the waters cover the deep. Sin, which has always caused so much trouble, will be done away with, and we will be free from all its sorrow and unhappiness. Then there will be no wars, no crime waves, no delinquency, and no hate. There will be only love, peace, and righteousness everywhere.

Even now, what a wonderful sensation it gives us to be at our best and to feel good and know that everything is going well! In that future time, with great happiness and joy mortals and immortals will work together in the temples to perfect their family relationships and complete the other necessary work pertaining to the salvation of the human family. During this one-thousand-year period, children will be born, grow up, marry, and live to old age. Then they will pass through a change equivalent to death and resurrection in the twinkling of an eye. Crops will be planted, harvested, and eaten; industries will be expanded; great cities will be built; education will be fostered; men will continue to care for their own needs, handle their own affairs, and enjoy the full blessings of their God-given free agency. Through the prophet Zephaniah, the Lord has said that he will give us a pure language. We will live in a state of peace, happiness, harmony, and beauty beyond our fondest imaginations. We will have a part in the government and will be priests and kings unto God and will reign with him for a thousand years. What a great time this will be to be alive, and what a challenging thought that we may help to bring this condition about!

About the time following this period, John the Revelator says, "And when the thousand years are expired, Satan shall be loosed out of his prison, and shall go out to deceive the nations which are in the four quarters of the earth, Gog and Magog, to gather them together to battle: the number of whom is as the sand of the sea (Revelation 20:7-8).

Then will come the great battle in which Satan shall be cast out forever; then will come the end of our earth as we now know it; then will come God's final judgment upon all men. John said:

> And I saw a new heaven and a new earth: for the first heaven and the first earth were passed away; and there was no more sea.
> And I John saw the holy city, new Jerusalem, coming down from God out of heaven, prepared as a bride adorned for her husband.
> And I heard a great voice out of heaven saying, Behold, the tabernacle of God is with men, and he will dwell with them, and they shall be his people, and God himself shall be with them, and be their God.
> And God shall wipe away all tears from their eyes; and there shall be no more death, neither sorrow, nor crying, neither shall there be any more pain: for the former things are passed away.
> And he that sat upon the throne said, Behold, I make all things new.
> He that overcometh shall inherit all things; and I will be his God, and he shall be my son. (Revelation 21:1-5, 7.)

After the earth's Millennium the work of our world will have been completed. Satan will be disposed of forever—the final judgments will have been made, and the earth will again be raised in status, this time to a celestial sphere, and it will become the permanent abode of those who are qualified as celestial beings. About this situation the Lord has said in our own day: ". . . he that endureth in faith and doeth my will, the same shall overcome, and shall receive an inheritance upon the earth when the day of transfiguration shall come; when the earth shall be transfigured, even according to the pattern which was shown unto mine apostles upon the mount; of which account the fulness ye have not yet received" (D&C 63:20-21).

The celestial order of life is that order to which God himself belongs. When Charles W. Penrose was a member of the First

Presidency of the Church, he wrote an article about this earth's role as the celestial abode of those worthy to live here. He said:

> The earth will die like its products but it will be quickened again and resurrected to celestial glory. It had been born of the water and will also be born of the Spirit, purified by fire from the corruption that once defiled it, developed into its perfections as one of the family of worlds, fit for the Creator's presence. All its latent light awakened into scintillating action, it will move up into its place among the orbs governed by celestial time shining like a sea of glass, mingled with fire, every tint and color of the heavenly bow radiating from its surface.
>
> The ransomed of the Lord will dwell upon it. The highest beings of the ancient orbs will visit it. The Garden of God will again adorn it. The heavenly government will prevail in every part. Jesus will reign as its king. The river of life will flow from the regal throne. The tree of life whose leaves were for the healing of the nations will flourish upon the banks of the heavenly stream, and its golden fruit will be free for the white-robed throngs that they may eat and live forever. This perfected earth with its saved inhabitants will then be presented to the Eternal Father as the finished work of Christ.

Orson Pratt said:

> Who, in looking upon the earth as it ascends in the scale of the universe, does not desire to keep pace with it? Then when it shall be cleansed and take its place among the dazzling orbs of the blue vault of heaven, shining forth in all of the splendors of celestial glory, he may find himself proportionately advanced in intellectual and moral excellence. O man, remember the future destiny and glory of the earth, and secure thine everlasting inheritance upon it, that when it shall be glorious you may be glorious also.

And again we might say, "What a great time to be alive!"

Index